BE THAT TEACHER WHO MAKES A DIFFERENCE

&

*Lead Aboriginal Education
For All Students*

KYLIE CAPTAIN   Dr CATHIE BURGESS

First published by Ultimate World Publishing 2022
Copyright © 2022 Kylie Captain & Cathie Burgess

ISBN

Paperback: 978-1-922828-71-2
Ebook: 978-1-922828-72-9

Kylie Captain & Cathie Burgess have asserted their rights under the Copyright, Designs and Patents Act 1988 to be identified as the authors of this work. The information in this book is based on the authors experiences and opinions. The publisher specifically disclaims responsibility for any adverse consequences which may result from use of the information contained herein. Permission to use information has been sought by the authors. Any breaches will be rectified in further editions of the book.

All rights reserved. No part of this publication may be reproduced, stored in or introduced into a retrieval system, or transmitted in any form, or by any means (electronic, mechanical, photocopying, recording or otherwise) without the prior written permission of the authors. Any person who does any unauthorised act in relation to this publication may be liable to criminal prosecution and civil claims for damages. Enquiries should be made through the publisher.

Layout and typesetting: Ultimate World Publishing
Editor: James Salmon
Book cover image: Michael Fardon

Ultimate World Publishing
Diamond Creek,
Victoria Australia 3089
www.writeabook.com.au

For all the educators who entered the profession to make a difference, and the Aboriginal support staff and community members who support the work we do.

You are valued and appreciated.

ACKNOWLEDGMENT OF COUNTRY

We acknowledge and pay respect to the Traditional Custodians and Elders of Country. We thank them for allowing us to live, work on and visit their spiritual lands. We acknowledge that these lands were never ceded, and that Australia is, was and will always be Aboriginal Country.

DISCLAIMER

This book contains the opinions of the authors. They acknowledge that readers may have differing opinions and beliefs. The strategies used and suggested by the authors do not intend to replace professional advice or research. Testimonies written in this book are the opinions of the individual and not the organisation they represent.

CONTEXT

We wrote this book to inspire and motivate teachers who support the learning of young people in schools. We do however acknowledge the role that families and communities play in educating their children. They are and will always be the first teachers.

In this book, we use the word Aboriginal, respectfully including Torres Strait Islander people, as we are located in New South Wales on the east coast of the Australian mainland where the term Aboriginal is commonly used by the peak Aboriginal organisation that provides advice to education departments. The NSW Aboriginal Education Consultative Group (AECG), and all policies and syllabuses in NSW use this terminology. The Aboriginal flag is an official flag of Australia and is widely recognised as representing the people, the sun, the land and the blood spilt defending the land. It is flown at key events, on important structures such as the Harbour Bridge and is front and centre of the fight for justice, equity and a seat at the table. In saying this, it is now common practice to recognise the land and/or language group of the local people.

We use the term Country (Aboriginal English - different from Standard Australian English), as one that describes land as a living entity, the essence of Aboriginality and includes relational connection to people, culture, spirituality, history, environment and ecologies of the non-human world.

Kylie lives and works on Dharawal Country and Cathie lives on Bideagal Country and works on Gadigal Country. Knowing the land or Country where you live and work is important and should be included in your Acknowledgement of Country. It's becoming common practice in workplaces, on airlines and in the media to see and hear an Acknowledgement of Country. This gives us hope that we are moving forward as a nation. There is still much more to be done and we're excited about the incredible things we'll see in the future.

ABOUT THE ARTIST

Campbelltown-based Aboriginal artist Michael Fardon holds a Bachelor of Visual Arts from the University of Western Sydney. Michael is a Dharawal man and self-taught artist who lives and works on Country using a range of styles and mediums, including painting and digital formats. Michael works closely with communities and schools to create collaborative mural art with Aboriginal students.

TESTIMONIALS

Teaching is the most noble of all professions. Emotionally strong, empathetic and compassionate teachers, such as Kylie Captain and Dr Cathie Burgess, are present in the lives of every successful human soul. They are special people who connect across and between cultures and class, who genuinely see the students who come under their gaze rather than just the pain and anguish of uncertainty that all students carry with them.

Emotionally strong, empathetic and compassionate teachers look below the surface and search for the hidden essence of their students because they understand that they are not simply educating and awakening their charges to a world of wonder and imagination but that they are also helping to grow and develop a human spirit, intellectually and emotionally.

As is the case with all professions, some of those who find their way to teaching soon realise that they are misplaced and so seek other career options better suited to their goals and aspirations. But when emotionally strong, empathetic and compassionate teachers connect with students, their impact is profound and lifelong, resulting in truly making a difference in the lives of students.

Read this important book and be empowered by its teachings. It serves as a guide for all those who seek to make a difference in the lives of young developing minds and souls. Strive to become that emotionally strong, empathetic and compassionate teacher. The rewards are endless.

Kylie Captain and Dr Cathie Burgess's book, 'Be that Teacher Who Makes a Difference & Lead Aboriginal Education For All Students' illustrates the power of emotionally strong, empathetic and compassionate teaching and its role in educating empathetic souls who are critical to creating and sustaining a world that is culturally responsive, respectful and socially equitable.

This book will help you connect with your students in stimulating and transformative ways so that one day a bright-eyed student will stand before you and tell you that they are happy that you are their teacher.

Professor Bob Morgan
Respected Aboriginal Educator, Researcher and Social Justice Advocate

Understanding how to be that teacher who makes a difference is one of the greatest aspirations of teachers. Yet not only is this is a difficult to learn how to do, it is notoriously difficult to explain. This new book takes up this challenge, giving its readers the gift of many years of experience and deep insight in Aboriginal Education. My congratulations and thanks to Kylie Captain and Cathie Burgess for giving this book to us, so that we too can learn how to be that teacher who makes a difference.

Valerie Harwood
Professor of Sociology and
Anthropology of Education
The University of Sydney

Kylie's story demonstrates the power a teacher can have in igniting a student's self-belief and determination. Her infectious energy and thirst for imparting knowledge is truly awe-inspiring.

I recommend this book to anyone who is restless in wanting to expand their sphere of influence and draw upon the gifts it contains to be the teacher who makes a difference and authentically leads Aboriginal Education for all students.

Kathy Powzun
Educational Leader

I first met Cathie at Clevo High School in the '80s when she was fresh out of teaching college. She was my Aboriginal Studies teacher and us Koori Kids immediately knew she was deadly, even back then. Her advocacy, energy, and determination to make a difference for us shone through. She challenged the systems, the racism and the inequality experienced by Aboriginal students on a daily basis. She earned her stripes in our communities and many Elders held her in such high regard.

Fast forward 40 years and her work, reputation, consistency, and stubbornness continue to make a difference for Aboriginal Education in the work she does with her student teachers at the University of Sydney.

As a community worker, I've had the pleasure of working alongside Cathie for a few years now in her Learning from Country program where Truth Telling is the focus. The relationships she has with Aboriginal organisations, Community Elders, Leaders, and workers across the state is testimony in itself to her incredible work. She not only teaches her students but practices what she teaches. Probably one of my most favourite sayings of Cathie's that she says to her Learning from Country students is 'you cannot unhear these stories'. This is so powerful, as it challenges their worldview and inspires change.

Julie Welsh
Aboriginal Community Facilitator
Culturally Nourishing Schooling Project UNSW

When you listen to Cathie Burgess talking about teaching you very quickly give her your full attention. Here is someone, you quickly realise, who has been there, done that and who very much knows what she is talking about - qualities that are all the more valuable in the field of Aboriginal education in which she has immersed herself throughout her working life.

Cathie also has that quality that is evident in all good teachers: a sense of humour. She doesn't pull any punches when she tells it like it is in the classroom but she will make even the most battle-wearied among us chuckle as she does so. To paraphrase the title of one of her chapters in this book: she has a bag full of tricks to help us on what can sometimes be a hard and rough trip to deadly teaching.

We could all go on and on about Cathie and what makes her a great teacher and an enormous asset to Aboriginal education - her years of experience; her long term engagement in the Aboriginal community; her dedicated service to organisations like the AECG and the ASA.

But time and space won't allow me to go into all of them. So let me just finish with a paragraph on one of these qualities: the very warm, very human touch she brings to her teaching and attempts to inculcate in all her teacher training students.

If you had to sum up the main things she wants us teachers to know about our craft I would say they were:
KNOW YOURSELF;
KNOW YOUR STUDENTS;
KNOW THEIR PARENTS.

However, she says that much better than me in her book when she writes: "remember that every student is someone's son or daughter and think about how you want people to treat your children".

No teacher will regret buying this book. Every teacher will gain from reading it.

Dr Paddy (Pat) Cavanagh
Poet and Historian
Honorary Life Member - AECG

Real stories, real scenarios and real strategies.

Here is a book that truly reflects honesty, experience and, above all, respect for Aboriginal Education by those who have been involved in it all their lives. The personal experience and narrative are from authors who have deep reverence and understanding of Aboriginal communities, their cultures and their beliefs.

Many educators still know very little about Aboriginal Peoples histories and cultures and are often dilatory to give it the proper inclusion that it deserves into their teaching learning programs.

The reader will be hard pressed to put this book down once the first pages become engrained in their own consciousness of what an educational journey in Aboriginal Education should be about.

A must source of inspiration for those who are just starting their teaching journey or for those who need further encouragement and understanding. Aboriginal Education is after all, everyone's business.

Dave Lardner
Former Aboriginal Education Consultant
and Project Officer

CONTENTS

Acknowledgment of Country	v
Disclaimer	vii
Context	ix
About the Artist	xi
Testimonials	xiii
Introduction	1
Chapter One: Kylie's Story	9
Chapter Two: Cathie's Story	35
Chapter Three: The Little Things That Make a Difference	55
Chapter Four: Teacher Wellbeing Makes a Difference	71
Chapter Five: Deep Listening Makes a Difference	81
Chapter Six: Cathie's Tips for Deadly Teaching	93
Chapter Seven: Fear of Getting It Wrong	105
Chapter Eight: From Surface to Deep Level Learning	121
Chapter Nine: Learning From Country	139
Chapter Ten: Pedagogy That Makes a Difference	161
Chapter Eleven: Resources and Where to Start	171
Chapter Twelve: Lead Aboriginal Education and Make a Difference	183
Summary	197
About the Authors	209
Want More?	213
Further Testimonials	215
Acronyms	221
Works by Dr Cathie Burgess	225
References	231

INTRODUCTION

> *"People will forget what you said, people will forget what you did, but people will never forget how you made them feel."*
> *- Maya Angelou.*

This book is for teachers and educators who want to make a difference. It's to give hope to and inspire those who may struggle with a system that is overworked, overwhelmed and under-resourced and where the passion and the 'why' is sometimes difficult to see.

Every human that walks this earth is shaped in one way or another by a teacher. A teacher who entered the profession to make a difference.

We hope to take you on a journey through our yarns and shared ideas to inspire and/or provide you with new knowledge. We do this because we are dedicated and passionate educators who want to make a difference. What better way than to write a book that we hope will help you on your journey of learning and being the best possible version of yourself.

Every child in Australian schools is required to obtain an education. Parents excitedly and nervously send their children off to school to commence kindergarten, often emotional and overwhelmed about all their child will experience and the challenges they may face over the next 13 years of schooling.

Some will have the most amazing experience. They cruise through with very few issues; however, there are many who struggle with learning and the challenges that come with schooling from social, cultural and academic perspectives.

Every child deserves an education and, importantly, the experience of knowing and feeling that a teacher believes in them, sees their potential and brings out the best in them. For those who have 'that teacher', it's hard to describe. Knowing someone cares deeply about your learning and wellbeing is comforting. Teachers have this incredible ability to build confidence and support students to grow into creative and confident learners and, importantly, good humans.

Teachers are passionate and dedicated professionals. Many things are out of their control, such as the number of students in classrooms, the lack of resources, the varying behaviours and trauma children come to school with, and the parents they interact with daily. It's a profession that takes courage and determination.

Throughout this book, we share our varied experiences and expertise to shine a light on the little things that make a difference, as it's these little things that shape and change lives.

Teachers are tired and under-resourced and have worked tirelessly through the COVID-19 pandemic to ensure students continue to learn and feel supported during this unprecedented time.

We wrote this book to remind all teachers that you are valued and needed. We hope to remind you of your worth and the reason you chose the incredible profession of teaching.

Great teachers lead from a place of passion and purpose, and every teacher comes into the profession with the same 'why'… to make a difference.

It's not easy. You are required to teach, coach, inspire, counsel, and be a friend and a mediator. You didn't choose an easy profession to embark on; it's one that requires you to continue to learn, reflect and grow.

If this book has landed in your hands, there is a reason you are reading it. There's a message you need to hear at this time in your life or career. It could be to remind you that you're inspiring and valued, or perhaps it's to give you a few tips to reignite your passion. Whatever it is, we thank you for coming on this journey with us.

When we decided to co-author this book, we saw it as a unique opportunity to share our similar passion and ideas around the little things that make a difference when teaching and leading Aboriginal education for all students - two topics that are close to our hearts and topics we feel deserve more attention, passion and enthusiasm.

We hope that you'll be inspired to try something new in order to motivate and get the best out of your students. We want to remind you that YOU are just as important as the students you teach. To ensure you are the best version of yourself, you have to take care of YOU first and foremost.

An important topic we explore throughout this book is Aboriginal education. We've come a long way in terms of how this is taught in Australian schools, however there is still so far to go. Some schools and educators are doing an incredible job, while others are just starting on their journey. Wherever you're at, we want to thank you for making it a priority. It doesn't matter how many Aboriginal students are in your school and whether you've had the opportunity to learn the history and culture yourself, the topic is important for all students. It's not black history or white history, it's our shared Australian history and important for all.

This book is important because for far too long, the education system has failed many. Adults report the negative experiences from school and the detrimental impact certain words had on them – sadly, many of those words came from a teacher.

There are others who report that they are who they are because a teacher believed in them.

We often meet people in varying professions who blame their education on the fact that they don't know the history of our country. Many say they learnt about Captain Cook and the experiences of the convicts and never about the Aboriginal peoples who have lived and nurtured this land for tens of thousands of years. It makes us sad that we continue to hear these stories.

It stops with us (we hope). Collectively, let's never allow another cohort of students to pass through our education system without knowing the truth of our country and about the rich and beautiful culture.

The unique and beautiful thing about this book is that we share our lived experiences from Aboriginal and non-Aboriginal perspectives and educators at varying stages in our careers.

Kylie was a student who struggled with school; she was absent a lot and had many challenges in her younger years. She didn't have aspirations for the future and didn't feel she was good enough or smart enough to achieve.

Cathie was that teacher who made a difference. She saw Kylie when she walked through the school gates, she interacted with her and did and said things that sparked a love of learning and self-belief that enabled her to not only successfully achieve her Higher School Certificate (HSC), but to complete a university degree to train as a primary school teacher.

Kylie is now an inspirational leader who inspires countless numbers of teachers and leaders to reflect on and improve their practice to ensure all students have access to a culturally safe and inclusive curriculum; one that allows Aboriginal students to see themselves in the curriculum and hopefully have a teacher who sees their potential and ignites a passion for learning. Kylie is passionate about ensuring every student obtains an education that will allow them to have a life of freedom and choice.

Cathie has had an incredible career in education – over 40 years' experience in teaching and leading Aboriginal education. She's an Associate Professor at The University of Sydney and has made a difference in the lives of many students and educators. She has led the way as a non-Aboriginal woman advocating for a socially just and equitable system to teach Aboriginal education truthfully, respectfully and importantly, for all.

Throughout this book, we touch on topics such as the power of education, the transformational power of strengths-based relationships, Aboriginal education for all and importantly, teacher wellbeing.

We share yarns about connecting with community and a shared approach to teaching with families, whilst recognising the importance that parents and communities play in their students' career aspirations and how working together can bring about transformational change.

We shine a light on curriculum and use a strengths-based approach to ensure that Aboriginal education is not just the responsibility of one person in a school but a priority of the entire school community and embedded in improvement plans and strategic goals.

We hope to inspire every educator and member of the school community, regardless of their position, to do their part to change lives, teach from a place of truth, passion and purpose and lead with courage.

Introduction

Join us on this journey of change - we need you, and our future generations need you.

Allow yourself to be vulnerable and courageous. The Reconciliation Australia and NAIDOC themes for 2022 as we write this book are Be Brave, Make Change and Get Up, Stand Up, Show Up, and we're asking you to do just that.

Start slow and do it well.

It takes a community – don't do it alone.

Learning and leading is fun when it links to your 'why' and it's even better when you can share this journey with others.

This is our story of being that teacher who makes a difference and leading Aboriginal education for all students.

Chapter One

KYLIE'S STORY

This collaboration between Cathie and I is an extension of the educational chapter shared in my first book *Dream Big & Imagine the What If*. Even though I trained as a primary school teacher and now support the improvement journey of schools and educators around Aboriginal education, my voice in this story is the voice of the student. Student voice is important and for the purpose of this book, I am reflecting on all the little things that made a difference for me. I'm lucky enough to be co-authoring with my high school teacher, the one who made a difference for me and who is now a colleague, friend and mentor. Cathie has had an incredible career in education with over 40 years of experience and countless stories from her students at the University of Sydney.

Together with our varied experience, we share from the perspective of the student and teacher as well as from the view of Aboriginal and non-Aboriginal educators - a pretty deadly and unique combo if you ask me.

We all have a story (chapter one in my first book). My story is one of resilience and hope. Hope to live a life of freedom and choice. If you've read my book or know my story, for the context of this book, I'm going to briefly re-cap it here for those who are learning about my journey for the first time.

I am a proud Gamilaroi woman. My Aboriginality has always been something I've been so proud of. From a very young age, my culture has made me feel strong and formed my identity. The connections, the laughs, the yarns with my mob and other blackfullas keeps me grounded.

My mob is from Walgett, a small country town in north-west New South Wales, where Mum Millie and Mum Denise were born and raised in a tin shack on the banks of the Namoi River. My family moved to Sydney to be closer to major hospitals as my birth mum Millie had a condition known as rhematic heart disease and issues with her valves. She sadly passed away at 28, when I was just three. Her sister, Mum Denise, then raised me as her own. I was lucky enough to have two mums and my beautiful Nan Delphine raise me to be the proud Aboriginal woman I am today. These three women have all passed now, however I carry their kindness, strength and resilience with me every day.

I grew up in Redfern and Waterloo, inner-city suburbs of Sydney where I spent the first 20 years of my life. I lived with Mum

Denise and her three daughters who became my sisters when Mum took me in. Growing up in Redfern and Waterloo in the '80s was tough; however, I have many fond memories of my childhood playing with friends, enjoying the basics of human connection before technology. We never had phones, so if I wanted to see if a friend was home, I'd have to walk over to their unit. Many of us lived in high-rise flats so we loved to get out and play in the local parks and wander the streets for fun.

We didn't have much; however, I wouldn't change it for a thing. Basic necessities were often hard to acquire for many of us living in public housing in a very low socio-economic area – very different to the hip place the streets of Redfern are today, where many gather to enjoy their soy and almond lattes and smashed avo on toast.

I didn't have aspirations or hopes for the future. I spent a lot of time in and out of hospital due to a chronic skin condition called psoriasis and was often absent from school. At 17, I had a near death experience and was diagnosed with a life-threatening heart condition, similar to my mum, which has required me to have three operations for my internal cardiac defibrillator. I'll live with this condition and device for the rest of my life. I'm grateful for the care I have received from my incredible cardiologist Dr Kuchar. As I write, I have just heard the devastating news of his passing. Dr Kuchar has been my cardiologist for the past 25 years. He was an intern working alongside Dr Victor Chang about 38 years ago who treated mum Millie. When I had my near death experience at 17, he recognised the name and couldn't help but put his hand up to treat and support me. He told me how much I was like my mum. Over the years, we developed a beautiful relationship. I trusted him with my life through my three surgeries for my implanted cardiac defibrillator. I wouldn't allow any other doctors to work on me, and he always respected my wishes and was there every time. I'm so sad to hear of his passing. I can only express so much gratitude for the love and care he provided over the past 25 years and for keeping me safe and healthy.

Like many Aboriginal families, we'd travel to and from the country for cultural obligations and to support family members when needed. These gaps in my attendance impacted on my performance and confidence at school.

I didn't ever think I was good enough or smart enough. I didn't see myself in the curriculum and I wasn't exposed to role models who ignited passion or dreams of a life I desired. I would have loved to hear about the authors, business owners and teachers but the stereotypical nature of the media always highlighted the athletes, artists or musicians who were deadly, but that wasn't me – I wasn't interested in or good at any of those things. I believe our kids need to see what they aspire to be, so it's important that we highlight the many deadly Aboriginal people who are out there doing incredible jobs and making a difference for their families and communities as there are many.

I started using drugs at 13 and by 14, I was heavily addicted. All the drug dealers around Waterloo and Redfern knew me. I struggled with severe addiction right throughout my teens and was living a life of drugs and crime. I'm not proud of my past. I share only to demonstrate that there is always a chance to change and redirect. Those who know me are often shocked when they hear of my past. They see me as the highly professional woman I am. Many have heard my story and have decided to put some extra effort and energy in to believing in their students and opening their minds to the possibilities of their future. This is the reason I share my story.

Cathie and the teachers at my school never gave up on me. All students should have someone to believe in them and see their potential.

The grief and sadness I've experienced throughout my life has been heartbreaking. When I reflect, it often seems unfair. I am, however, a resilient woman who lives with a grateful heart by choosing to focus on the good. To look after myself, I do a lot of inner work to help me stay focussed and live from a place of gratitude. There are always people who have had it worse than me and for this reason, I choose to focus on all the wonderful things in my life.

All of my experiences have shaped me into the woman I am today.

I am a proud Aboriginal woman, a passionate educator who has survived many of life's assignments. I am also an intergenerational survivor of the many horrific injustices that have been placed on my people for generations. I hope it stops with me.

I do my best to give hope to inspire and motivate others.

Throughout my book, *Dream Big & Imagine the What If,* I share some of those 'what if' moments that have shaped me into the strong, proud, resilient woman I am today.

I try to flip those 'what if's' which are often negative and encourage the reader to imagine the 'what if' in a positive light.

I am proud of my culture. My Aboriginality is where I draw my strength and resilience. The feelings of pride, culture, spirituality and connection keep me strong as I come from a long line of resilient and deadly people. If they could survive through many of life's struggles and assignments, so can I.

The Lightbulb Moments That Made the Difference

In 1996, as a 15-year-old and in Year 10, I was a student with no hopes or dreams. I was heavily addicted to drugs, trying to hold on for as long as I could in the hope of achieving my Year 10 Certificate. I didn't think that I had the ability to go on to attain my HSC, however, at a very critical point in my life I recall a few moments that changed my life and attitude towards education and aspirational life goals.

It was a teacher (there were a few actually). I make special mention to Ms Burgess as these are the lightbulb moments. Those pivotal times in life that stand out. I play these moments over and over in my head and express so much gratitude for them. They are the little things that made a difference for me and changed the trajectory of my life.

I wasn't an engaged learner. There were times when I didn't want to go to school. I recall being sent to the hospital to attend special reading programs and always felt like I was behind the rest of the class. I'd often sit in the back of class quietly, wishing I was invisible so that the teacher wouldn't call on me to answer any questions. I went to school because I had to and for the social interaction.

I recall walking in the school gates and into the office to get my late note as I was always late. I'd usually rock in around 10:30 or 11 am. I remember bumping into my teacher, Ms Burgess, who always lit up every time she saw me. She was often busy rushing from class to class with books and papers in her hands, but every time she saw me, she stopped to acknowledge me and ask how I was going. I recall these moments so vividly because of the way she made me feel. She'd say, "I can't wait to see you in my Aboriginal Studies class next year", "You're going to be amazing". She said it every time I saw her.

I recall these moments because, at the time, I had no intention of being in her class the following year. My goal at that point was to try my best to hang on for as long as I could as I was so close to dropping out. I was hoping to attain my Year 10 certificate like my sister Narelle who I looked up to. I thought that if Narelle could make it to the end of Year 10, then I could too. The thought of staying on for another two years wasn't an option that crossed my mind.

Narelle sadly passed away when she was just 30 years old. I continue to express gratitude to her for being my inspiration. Narelle's infectious smile and love of life is part of my story. I learnt so much from my beautiful sister and I'm forever grateful for having her in my life. I'm glad I could repay her by becoming a carer for her 12 year old son when I was aged just 21. That's how I see life, you receive, you give and it keeps going around – that's the wonderful thing about life.

Ms Burgess's words and the way she made me feel did something that ignited a spark within me. I remember thinking, "What if she's right?" and "What if I could be the first in my family to attain the HSC?" Fast forward a few years later and she was right. I did get my HSC and with her support, I did exceptionally well. Aboriginal Studies was my favourite subject. For the first time, I saw myself in the curriculum. The intergenerational trauma, stories and sadness of our history suddenly made sense. I started to understand why my mum had an issue with white people and why she never felt comfortable coming to my school.

Ms Burgess and her belief in me changed my life. I genuinely felt supported and believed her when she said I could do it.

I was the first person in my family to attain my HSC, and the first to complete a university degree. I have achieved more than I could ever have dreamt possible – home ownership and investing, world travel, health, career and personal goals such as writing a book. I have achieved such success because I decided to back myself and my ability to achieve. I decided to dream big and imagine the 'what if'. I turned that fear into resilience and have been setting goals and backing myself ever since.

Another critical moment was when my Careers Advisor, Ms Mander-Ross organised for me to complete my work experience at the Department of Aboriginal Affairs. This was another lightbulb moment and one I think of often and express so much gratitude for. Without this experience, I genuinely feel that my life would have taken a very different direction. I'm so thankful that my school focussed on my strengths and linked me with something that would engage me as they knew how much I loved my culture and how proud I was to be Aboriginal.

They organised for me to spend one week with the Department of Aboriginal Affairs, learning all aspects of the organisation. My school took care of any barriers that prevented me from attending, such as arranging for a bus pass which allowed me to travel in and out of the city without having to pay. They also organised a $50 gift voucher, so I could buy some work clothes as I didn't have any or the money to buy them myself.

I remember this moment so clearly, and more importantly, how it made me feel.

I nervously took the bus from Waterloo into the city and rocked up to Wynyard with all the other morning commuters hurrying quickly through the city. I looked up at those tall buildings and felt nervous.

I decided to be brave and took those first steps and entered that building. I loved every minute of my experience. I had the opportunity to work in all the different sections of the department, from admin to family history research and reception. I was in my element and loving life. That was the first week that I'd ever committed to anything and showed up on time every day. They asked my school if I could stay on for another week as I was doing such a great job and encouraged me to stay at school and get my HSC. My school was supportive of their request as they were beyond proud that I was attending and doing well.

From that moment, I knew what I wanted to do. To work for an organisation that helped my people. That experience changed my life and showed me that Aboriginal people could be successful in many different careers. I remember going home to Mum telling her about the deadly blackfullas working in the city and all of the incredible opportunities. I honestly didn't know they were there.

In 1998, I was the first person in my family to complete the HSC. It was such a proud moment for Mum, who was there at graduation to watch me receive my certificate and win awards for outstanding achievement. Prior to this she never liked coming to school because of her own experience.

Mum wasn't allowed to go to school from the age of 11. She was out working on cattle stations for white families. Back then, that's how things were for many Aboriginal families. Mum wasn't a citizen of this country until she was 15. She grew up with the horrific policies and discrimination that many Aboriginal families experienced. This impacted on her trust in white people and government organisations. I did my best to break down the barriers and tell her yarns about Ms Burgess and other deadly teachers, so she would know there were many who were there to walk alongside and support our people. Having Mum there at my graduation was one of the best moments of my life. In my mind, I can still see her smiling up real proud and hear the pride in her voice as she told everyone in our community about my achievement.

Following the completion of my HSC, I was sent many offers to study at university. I accepted an offer to study teaching at the University of Sydney. I knew I wanted to be a teacher. I am a very reflective person and I often sit and give thanks to the people who have supported my journey.

Cathie and other teachers did an amazing job and so did the deadly Aboriginal staff at school. I'm forever grateful for the Aboriginal Education Officers who were there for me and have continued to be there for countless other Aboriginal students over the years. The same staff who were there then, are still there now making a difference and supporting our kids and communities. I need to give a special shoutout to Uncle Hilton and Aunty Linda as they went above and beyond to support so many of us kids. They were always there with a smile, a feed if needed and a culturally safe space to sit and yarn. Aunty Deb and the many other Aboriginal staff in schools do such a deadly job. Their support makes a difference and they deserve recognition for the incredible work they do in shaping and changing lives.

Throughout my career, Cathie and I have remained in contact. I didn't complete my teaching degree on my first attempt. It just wasn't meant to be. I dropped out a few months after I started and fell back into old habits of smoking drugs and going nowhere in life. I then miraculously landed a traineeship with the Department of Aboriginal Affairs which was another turning point that helped steer me in the right direction.

Things then took another turn as I fell pregnant at 18 and had my son at 19. I was a stay at home mum for two years before I embarked on a career as a Customer Service Specialist at St George Bank for six years. I then secured a job supporting families and communities, which aligned with my passion and purpose. I loved working and everything about it. The friendships, the learning and the challenges shaped me into the woman I am today.

The thought of becoming a teacher never left my mind. I knew I'd get there one day. When my son was four, I had my second child so my main priority was to be the best mum I could be. I worked and raised my children with their dad. We had so much to be grateful for.

Life was cruising along smoothly. All the sadness and worries of my younger years seemed to be behind me as I devoted every waking moment to being the best mother and partner I could be. Life was good. I was beyond grateful for a chance to live and be happy. That's when everything changed. My world and life as it was turned upside down overnight as we were faced with the devastating news that Richard, my fiance and father of my children, suddenly passed away. It's a time and moment that broke my heart into a million pieces. I talk about the grief and experiences in my first book as throughout my many challenging times, I loved learning through other people's experiences of overcoming adversity. That's why I decided to write a book. I thought that perhaps someone may benefit from hearing my story and it's with much pride that I share that my story has made a difference for many. From professionals at all levels to first time readers. I continue to hear from people who thank me for sharing my story. This warms my heart, knowing that I've helped others.

Those who know me will describe me as resilient. I keep going despite all of the challenges that have been thrown my way. I'm thankful for my strength and resilience and to be here telling my story in hope to make a difference for others.

In the following years after Richard's passing, I worked hard to recreate a home and life for my children. I cried myself to sleep every night and held my babies tight praying and dreaming of peace and happiness. I didn't want them to suffer because of the tragic circumstances we were faced with. I continued to work and dreamt of being on the other side of the counter of the bank I once worked in. I didn't know any Aboriginal people who owned their own home. I wanted to set myself a goal so big, so that I knew if I achieved it, I could go on and achieve anything I set my mind to. My dream came true and within two years of Richard passing, I was back at my bank, applying for and being approved for a loan to buy my first home. It was one of my proudest moments as Mum Denise was there to see our home. She was so proud of me.

Sadly, not long after this, Mum was diagnosed with cancer and passed away. Life had yet again thrown me another devastating blow and I couldn't help but wonder why these terrible things kept happening.

I've lost so many loved ones. Both mums, my beautiful nan, my sister, a best friend, the father of my children and many more family and community members. I often wonder why some have to suffer while others cruise through life without such pain and sadness. It's a question I will never find the answers to. All I know is that as long as the sun is rising and setting each day, there is a chance to learn, grow and make a difference.

Reflecting on my loss again is heartbreaking but also healing, as sharing stories and allowing myself to be vulnerable gives me strength, knowing that my story has helped many.

Even after these devastating and life-changing experiences, the thought of becoming a teacher remained on my mind. As a single mum, I was then working full-time and raising my two young children who were busy with sport and dance. As much as I wanted to study, I truly didn't believe I would even survive my first assignment. I didn't think I was smart enough to pass, to be honest.

I remember feeling confident and inspired to take a chance on my study dream. I decided to email my good old friend and mentor Ms Burgess. It had been a while between emails so I'm sure she would have been surprised to hear from me. My email went something like this.

> "Dear Cathie, I hope you're well... As you know, I work full-time, and I'm raising my young kids, however I still have this dream of becoming a teacher. Do you reckon I could do it? I'd have to work full-time, study full-time and raise my kids. It seems like a lot."

She emailed me back with a very short and sharp email that said, *"Of course you can, you're smart, you can do it"*. She always makes things sound so easy. Because she made it sound easy, that's what I started to tell myself. I worked tirelessly after hours and on weekends during my four years of study. It was hard at times, but I got there and did extremely well at uni. Most years I ended up on the Dean's Merit List for outstanding academic achievement.

Who would have thought that I'd be here telling my story as a published author and educator? I often have to pinch myself in disbelief about how my life turned out. I truly do live a life of freedom and choice. I feel that I'm living a life that was written for someone else. I am an author, educator, homeowner and a world traveller. I am happily married and my children are now 22 and 18. One of my proudest moments as a mother was to watch them graduate with their HSC. I could go on for a few chapters telling you about my deadly husband and children, but I'll leave those yarns in my other book, or who knows, future books to come.

I don't see myself as a writer, just someone who has a few yarns to share. Those who know me know how much I like to yarn. My book has been reviewed by well known authors and has been described like sitting down having a cuppa while I share yarns. I use Aboriginal English throughout and I'm happy that I had the autonomy to write it the way I wanted to. I included chapters on the power of education, Aboriginal history and culture as well as my tips to living an abundant life – kind of like a motivational book (my favourite kind).

My writing journey hasn't been easy. I didn't do it for myself, I did it for the lives I could possibly impact. Mainly the lives of our young people. I want to let them know that it doesn't matter how many obstacles life may throw at them, there is always hope and someone or something there to help. I also wrote to encourage the teachers and adults to never stop believe in their young people. It doesn't matter how many times students have failed or been down the wrong path, there is always a chance to redirect and take the path less travelled.

I have found it hard to celebrate my achievements out of fear of judgement. Writing my book took me to a whole new level of vulnerability. The fear I experienced was terrifying. Fear of judgement, fear of failure and even fear of success. It's now 12 months since publishing and I'm only just starting to come down from the incredible high I was on. When I reflect on the past year, I can't help but smile. I smile with pride because of my courage but mostly I smile because of the thousands of people my book has helped. From principals, teachers to students and first-time readers. What makes me most happy is that blackfullas of all ages have been reading my book and feeling proud and inspired. The yarns shared and the Aboriginal English I use throughout has allowed them to see themselves within the text. I have received countless messages from people from across the country and aboard thanking me for sharing my story and all the tips and tricks that have helped me. My chapter Black and Proud has allowed me to shine a light on the history of this country and the rich and beautiful culture that we should all celebrate and be proud of.

Life will always have obstacles, but one thing I know for sure is that I am the creator of my destiny and the writer of my dreams.

What I Did That Made a Difference

There are many things I've done throughout my life that have led me to where I am now. I go into detail in my first book; however, I thought it would be important to highlight that success didn't happen by chance. Along with the little things Cathie and my school did for me, I have to give myself a little credit for the hard work and positive mindset I've developed along the way. I did work hard, and I refused to surrender to the circumstances that were thrown my way.

People often ask how I've managed to be so driven and goal-oriented despite the many challenges I've experienced. Along with the power of education, I attribute my success to the law of attraction and my ancestors guiding and protecting my journey. I seek their guidance and ask for the help and support I need. I set goals and create movies in my mind about all the things I hope to achieve.

It ignites this fire in my belly, and the motivation comes from within. I love having goals to work towards, whether they be personal goals, material goals or experiences. Many dreams haven't turned out. However, there is always a lesson to be learnt from those experiences.

I have always used my connection to culture as my greatest source of strength. My Aboriginality runs deep within my soul. My connection to my ancestors and family members who have passed is strong, and I often seek their spiritual guidance, love and support to help navigate my way through life. Knowing that I come from the longest-living surviving culture in the world, makes me proud and keeps me strong. Their resilience has been passed on to me and I tap into that strength when needed.

The law of attraction has also supported everything I have achieved in life. The law of attraction has become well known by the book and documentary *The Secret,* which has been used for thousands of years and by many of the world's most incredible scientists and changemakers. It may sound crazy to some; however, I believe in it. Having a positive mindset and working towards your dreams and goals can't do any harm.

The law of attraction is about living a positive life, visualising and seeing your thoughts and energy as magnets. Think positive thoughts and positive things come your way. Think negative, then that's what you'll attract.

The power of manifestation is life changing.

The Universe responds to the kinds of thoughts we think, and many of us have a way of limiting our thinking and beliefs to what we feel we are worthy of.

As Buddha said, *"What you think you become. What you feel you attract and what you imagine you create."*

Using the law of attraction is not easy and takes consistent work. I have not mastered it all; however, I know that when I commit and put my mind to it, it never fails.

Along with my goal setting which I break down into simple steps in my Dream Big Journal and free goal setting tool found on my website, I also make sure I live in the moment and take the time to give thanks for, appreciate and enjoy the here and now. An essential part of the law of attraction is gratitude. The more you are grateful, the more the Universe will give you to be grateful for. I can't go past one day without expressing gratitude for every blessing in my life. As I open my eyes each morning, knowing my family is healthy and safe, I give thanks. As I turn on the tap to clean drinking water, I give thanks, and as I drive, I give thanks to my guides and ancestors for protecting my journey.

The law of attraction is about visualising the outcome you want.

First, you must start to believe that anything is possible.

I have many yarns I can tell you about the law of attraction and how I've used it to attract experiences, people and things into my life. I elaborate in my book or if we ever have the chance to yarn, I'll happily tell you.

My dream has always been to live a fulfilling life, making a difference in the lives of others and I'm proud to say that in my 41 years so far, I have done just that.

Once I realised my potential, I thought, *"If I could achieve that dream, what else could I achieve?"*

I saw myself having these powers and knowledge that I should pass on to others.

I have dreamt up many things in my life and for as long as I live, I'll continue to be a dreamer.

I could go on and on.

To sum up the things that helped me, I would have to say:

- Connecting to culture
- Gratitude
- Journaling
- Goal setting
- Visualisation
- Having someone believe in me
- Healthy lifestyle
- Selecting my circle

- Rubbing shoulders with those who inspire me
- A growth mindset

I'm grateful for the life I live and the job I do in improving outcomes for Aboriginal students and inspiring teachers to never give up on their students.

I am who I am because someone believed in me.

Someone told me I was smart and deadly and could do anything I set my mind to. I'm lucky enough to be co-writing this book with her.

I embarked on a career in education because I feel it's where I can have the most impact. Gaining an education has the ability to change the trajectory of someone's life. It offers freedom and choice, something everyone should have. It was a few kind teachers who made a difference for me, so I think it's fitting that I pay it forward and do the same for other students.

I am the President of the Aboriginal Studies Association (ASA), where I continue to work alongside my incredible teacher and mentor, Ms Burgess. Ms Burgess now has the formal title of Dr Cathie Burgess as she is an Associate Professor at The University of Sydney. Cathie was the President of the ASA for 13 years and as a non-Aboriginal woman, has done an incredible job leading Aboriginal education and making a difference in the lives of the students and educators who have had the pleasure to learn from her. I was content with my role as Vice President, learning and growing as a leader until last year she said, "I think you'd be great as President". I was afraid as it sounded like a fancy title and a lot of responsibility, however once again, I decided to lean into the fear and trust her judgement once again. When will this woman stop?!

Cathie is often embarrassed when I share my yarns about her being that teacher who made a difference for me, however, I share these yarns because they're true. I share because I want every teacher to remember why they chose to become teachers and the transformational difference they can have on a student's performance at school. If a teacher believes a student can achieve, that's the first step in them actually achieving. Learning is hard and many students come to school with limiting beliefs in their ability. It's up to teachers to make learning fun and engaging whilst ensuring all of the learning styles are catered for.

As a leader in Aboriginal education, I support hundreds of teachers to reflect on and improve their practice, and I see the exhaustion and frustration in them. Their role requires them to do more than learn and teach content. They are so much more and the passion and commitment they bring to the profession often goes unnoticed. Teacher colleagues often report missing out on family events due to catching up on work and preparing lessons on weekends. Some even report going to sleep in the early hours of the morning due to the unbearable workload.

My Hopes and Dreams for This Book

My hope for this book is to reignite passion in our teachers as it's the energy and the way they make you feel that makes a difference. Cathie and I hope to share our yarns from both an Aboriginal and non-Aboriginal perspective and touch on topics such as teacher wellbeing, work/life balance, connecting with community and building the confidence and capacity of educators in Australian schools to do their part in ensuring Aboriginal education is taught well.

My dream is that every teacher who reads this book will join us on a journey of change. A change when there will no longer be a time that adults blame their education for their lack of understanding and knowledge about Australian history. We hope to develop the confidence of teachers to teach our history and rich and beautiful culture. We don't want them to teach from a black or a white perspective, we simply want them to teach the truth.

Sadly, our history has not been taught truthfully and authentically. While Australia has a sad history of colonisation and dispossession, we also have a history that dates back tens of thousands of years and one that is full of rich and beautiful culture for all to learn from and engage with.

It really is a surreal feeling to be co-authoring book number two with the incredible Dr Cathie Burgess. I'll continue to share our story and the difference she made for me and many others in hope my story may just encourage a teacher to change the way they interact with their students and do their part to unlock their hidden potential, just as Cathie did with me.

Without having a teacher who believed in me, I honestly don't feel that I would be living the life I have the privilege to live today. I feel that I would've ended up either in prison or dead because of the negative path I was heading down.

We hope this book will give educators confidence when teaching and leading Aboriginal education in their schools, but importantly to reignite that spark and passion and to remind them about why they chose teaching as a profession.

Teachers play an important role and we must never forget the incredible contributions they make.

When you reflect on your own schooling experience, I'm sure you will share with me in giving thanks to a teacher who had an impact on your life. Sadly, many people go on and achieve great success to prove a teacher wrong as some report that a teacher told them they would never amount to anything or that they didn't have the ability to achieve.

Teachers have this magical power to make or sometimes break a student's confidence. Our words and our energy in the way we teach and lead play a critical part in supporting student learning.

This book is important because we focus on relationships and human connections. We focus on the importance of leadership within a school community and the importance of leadership not being defined by the executive in the school or the position you hold. Leadership is defined by the actions you take and how you positively influence those around you.

We wrote this book because we believe anyone can become a leader. We need more leaders to spread positivity and uplift each other so that every student knows they are good enough and smart enough to achieve whatever it is they set their mind to.

As Muhammad Ali said, "If my mind can conceive it and my heart can believe it, then I can achieve it". As educators, there are times we need to motivate students to believe in their ability and to take risks in their learning in order for them to unlock their hidden potential and go on to live a life of freedom and choice.

To learn more about my story you can purchase a copy of *Dream Big & Imagine the What If* by visiting kyliecaptain.com.au

I've included a few of my favourite quotes below. I hope you enjoy.

> "You are the author of your story and
> the writer of your dreams."
> (Kylie Captain).

> "Every child deserves a champion, an adult who will never give up on them, who understands the power of connection, and insists that they become the best that they can possibly be."
> (Rita Pierson)

> "Owning our story and loving ourselves through that process is the bravest thing we'll ever do."
> (Brené Brown)

> "Nothing is impossible, the word itself says 'I'm possible'!"
> (Audrey Hepburn)

With sincere gratitude and appreciation for allowing me to share my story with you.

Your dreams are only a thought away – imagine the 'what if'.

END OF CHAPTER REFLECTION

What can you learn from Kylie's experience?

_____

_____

_____

Think about the students you could make a difference for. How would it make you feel if you could support their journey in education and life?

_____

_____

_____

_____

How does Kylie's story challenge you to reflect on your practice and little things you could do to make a difference for students?

_____

_____

_____

_____

_____

_____

_____

_____

_____

_____

_____

_____

Chapter Two

CATHIE'S STORY

Recently I went to an ex-student's 50th birthday – yes 50th – so this caused me to pause and reflect on how I ended up here!

I was one of those nerdy kids who loved reading which translated into wanting to become a teacher, even though I spent a lot of time in high school outside the classroom for talking too much! I even kept my social studies books from primary school because I thought that they would be good resources for when I became a teacher. Ironically, this proved to be the case but not for the reasons I thought – rather, I have used them as examples of inappropriate, inaccurate and racist materials that many of us grew up with and influenced our (mis)understanding of Aboriginal peoples, cultures and histories.

This story is also a story of the power of education to uplift, inspire, change and teach us critical lessons for life. My mum would have loved to have been a teacher but in the 1950-60s university fees were high, her mother couldn't afford it and women were expected to get married and raise their children from home, so that's what Mum did. She did however work as a teacher's aide in a high school and was an amazing and much-loved netball coach, coaching many representative sides to victory. She brought us three girls up to believe we could do and be anything, that we didn't have to get married and have kids if we didn't want to, and that a career was possible. I have Mum and Gough Whitlam to thank for the opportunity to become a teacher and do what I love every day. I still get excited when students I teach get more than just the content from class. When you know that you have changed the way they think and feel, that is when you know you are meant to be a teacher and I am grateful for every opportunity to be the best teacher I can be.

What I have learnt from working in many contexts is that as a teacher I am not always the expert, and in Aboriginal contexts, how little I knew, how racist many of the ideas I grew up with were, and how determined I became that future generations of kids would not grow up ignorant or racist. I had always been that typical proud Aussie and then here I was, suddenly ashamed of many aspects of our history and society. So I listened and learned from the first teachers of this country, Aboriginal people, and boy did they give me some tough lessons along the way, lessons I am now grateful for and lessons I am still learning.

I also learnt the importance of engaging with students, families and community members in non-judgmental, supportive and respectful ways, the criticality of mentors and mentoring – supporting and being supported by colleagues who get you – and acknowledging that everyone has something to contribute including the mad, the bad, the sad and the glad (as I colloquially refer to the many I have met along the way). Starting each day with a clean slate, and the gift of being a teacher and learner, in all its pain and glory, are also key to making a difference.

I grew up in working class inner west Sydney, which was the western suburbs in those days, so we were disdainfully tagged as 'westies', but that didn't impact me until I went to teachers' college on the North Shore. Suddenly it became apparent that we were pretty close to the bottom of the ladder, but I was 'saved' by the fact that I played a lot of sport and could add value to any team I joined. In fact, my first lecturing job was in a netball course for the PE department, even though I was primary/special education trained. Needless to say, the PE students were less than impressed!

Clevo Days

It was this training that resulted in my first teaching appointment to a large inner city Sydney high school (affectionately known as Clevo), then a poor, working class, multicultural area, well-known for its political activism and much-loved local football team, the South Sydney Rabbitohs. The appointment was a shock, as I had elected to go anywhere in NSW to teach primary school and here I was in the middle of the city at a high school. Apparently, my special education training meant I was appointed as a GA (general activities) teacher which essentially meant teaching basic literacy and numeracy skills until the students left at 15 or Year 10 – whichever came first. What this looked like in reality was that I ended up with all the kids none of the 'real' teachers wanted in their class and so I had mixed ability classes of largely Aboriginal and immigrant students, in the English department.

It was the early 1980s and Aboriginal kids were still largely placed in the bottom classes because it was assumed that they couldn't learn or that they weren't interested in education.

At least at Clevo, the Aboriginal population was acknowledged through a Koori room, Aboriginal Education Assistant (the terminology of the time) and an Aboriginal Resource Teacher, who largely supported the students and liaised with local Aboriginal families and the community. This was my first experience with teaching Aboriginal kids, even though I had gone to multicultural schools myself and did my prac teaching in similar schools. Ironically, I have Aboriginal cousins on my father's side by marriage and although we met a few times, we didn't really know them because they lived further west than we did. I certainly didn't make any connection between this family and what I had learnt about 'the Aborigines' at school.

Because I was the youngest and last appointed to the school at the time, I was given an Aboriginal project where I took half a dozen Year 9 Aboriginal kids to Murawina Aboriginal Preschool in Eveleigh Street Redfern (an infamous place where many Aboriginal families lived, now known as the Block). We visited one day a week to read to and write stories for the preschoolers. The area was well known for clashes with police who closely monitored the Aboriginal population, often locking locals up for minor offences, an ongoing source of media sensationalism and derision.

However, I was happy to be out of school with a chance to get to know these funny, vibrant (and sometimes exhausting) kids in a different context which was simultaneously new, exciting, and a little bit scary. I remember the first time I took them to the preschool and the Aboriginal Aunty who was running the place very sternly told me, "We don't like white people coming in here telling us what to do. We'll run the project our way." Well, I wasn't going to argue with that, and I quickly said, "Oh yeah, sure. I'm just the driver." It was also the first time I had been called 'white' and it baffled me, but I soon got used to it as it was regularly used, often alongside a number of creative expletives.

While the project was successful, a few teachers complained loudly about the kids missing class, so I wrote an Aboriginal Studies course so the students could do this work in class time and get marks for it. In those days schools could submit school-based courses for approval and implement them in ways that best suited their students and context (the good old days). So I wrote this course completely from a local community's current (rather than historical) point of view because I was, if nothing else, aware of my complete lack of knowledge in the subject.

What I did know though was that there was plenty of knowledge and expertise in our local community, and we just needed to tap into this and see where it led us. Looking back, it was an insane leap of faith, but the students, their families and the community came together, and along with a history teacher who was doing a similar Year 11 course, we managed to pull off some pretty innovative and engaging experiences for the kids as well as ourselves. We were also lucky that many of the students had family members running complex Aboriginal organisations or working in interesting jobs who willingly contributed their expertise and experiences with the class.

So, we started up a newsletter called the 'Clevo Koori Newsletter' full of student and community work and experiences which quickly went around the state. We made connections with rural schools and took the kids on excursions to expose them to new and different experiences. Like everything innovative to come out of schools, it eventually became institutionalised as a new syllabus, but at least it maintained its largely current and community focus.

I also learned (by accident if I'm honest) the importance of sport in the local Aboriginal community where extended family and community members played together, were successful and looked up to for their success. While still not level, the playing field of sport was closer than most other spheres of life and the focus on the team effort was more in line with Aboriginal values.

As I grew up playing, umpiring and coaching sport, I enthusiastically got involved in school sport, and sometimes watched the kids play at Redfern and Waterloo oval on the weekends. And so, through sport, I was able to get to know the kids and their families, not as a teacher but as a person, which again was a bit scary at first.

I remember once I had this kid in my class who was hard work and disruptive most of the time. He came running over towards me at the footy on the weekend and I thought, "Oh my God, why am I here on the weekend? Why am I putting myself through this? I don't need it on the weekend." Anyway, he came running over to me and said, *"Hi miss, come and meet my mum, and my aunty and my nan"*. Much to my surprise, he introduced me to all his family, and we just started chatting about the footy. It was such a shock. Outside of school he was this great kid from a big family and was very respectful to community people and so I saw this whole different kid. Then the following week at school, he was a lot less naughty. He would often say, *"Oh, miss, it was so much fun seeing you at the footy"* and we'd talk about it and he'd settle down and do his work. So what I learned early on is the positive effects of getting to know kids and their families outside of school.

Make no bones about it though, it was a stressful place to work, and I wouldn't have made it without the close friends I made who were also surviving teaching on a day-to-day basis. We were a work hard, play hard cliché, not much older than the students we taught and not well-prepared for this experience by our teacher training. I was also lucky to have a reading support teacher, Bev Williams, who taught me how to teach and protected me when I got into trouble from the powers that be (which was often). Without Bev, I don't think I would have made it through my first few years of teaching.

I feel I was very lucky that this was my first school as it not only taught me a lot about teaching, learning and schools, but about people, cultures, the importance of belonging, resilience and perseverance, as well as the devastating effects of poverty and alienation on families and communities – an unforgivable and preventable failure of governments and systems. This also made me determined to use education to try and break down these barriers for kids and their families.

A White Woman Working in a Black World

After leaving Clevo, I had a short stint selling computers in a local computer shop, where it became obvious that I wasn't made for sales as I was giving away too many freebies to parents buying their kid's first computer. I wasn't ready to go back to teaching, and so was lucky enough to get a job at the Western Sydney University (Macarthur Institute at the time) as the Aboriginal Rural Education Program Coordinator. The program was about getting mainly mature-aged Aboriginal people from rural and remote areas into a teaching or social work degree.

The idea of the program is that these areas are hard to staff and often have large Aboriginal populations, so it seems logical to train locals into these positions as they have a deeper understanding of the context and are more likely to stay there for a long time. My job was to recruit Aboriginal people into the program by visiting these communities, as well as organise logistics such as travel and accommodation for students coming to university on intensive block-mode study weeks.

I was out of my depth as a non-Aboriginal person working in a largely Aboriginal environment with no experience in rural or remote Aboriginal communities. I was very lucky to have some fantastic Aboriginal mentors who taught me about Aboriginal community protocols and supported me when I made inevitable mistakes and inadvertently offended someone. I learned an awful lot about our country, such as how the colonial frontier was still alive and operating in overt and covert ways. In many rural towns, racism was right there in your face - you could feel it, hear it and see it as you drove into town and because you were meeting with Aboriginal people, you became highly aware of its existence.

I also learned a lot about the diversity of Aboriginal communities and saw many Aboriginal-led innovative programs designed to address the needs of their communities, programs and strategies that received little attention or credit beyond their community despite their innovation and success.

The power of education to transform lives was again evident and many graduates have gone on to be leaders in their community as well as in education.

By then I was ready to go back to teaching and randomly ended up at one of the top selective high schools in the state, as it was the only position my profile matched. I was the technology teacher (a story for another time that my kids still laugh about), which while interesting, was not as exciting as the Aboriginal Studies classes I taught. This was the first HSC Aboriginal Studies course available state-wide and the non-Aboriginal students who selected it were either passionate and committed to making change or were rebelling against their parents. Either way, they were great kids to work with and many received the top marks in the state in Aboriginal Studies and other subjects, going onto university to do law, environmental science, media and communications etc.

We went to the Northern Territory with my partner's Uncle, a traditional owner from central Australia. This was an interesting and crazy trip where, at one point, the students staged a protest about racist actions by a checkout worker at a grocery store. We flew the Aboriginal flag for NAIDOC and never took it down – making the front page when Cathy Freeman carried the Aboriginal flag around the Commonwealth Games stadium – and we worked out a way to run Aboriginal Studies classes outside of school when the school prevented the course from continuing.

I learnt several lessons from this experience, not least of which was how to strategise and work around the power brokers. I developed a keen eye for detail as accountability and parental pressure was on a whole new level there. I learned how to stimulate, provoke, engage and facilitate learning for gifted kids, and saw the significance of Aboriginal Studies in developing passion and purpose in non-Aboriginal students to make a difference. Recently, an ex-student turned up as the lawyer on a friend's Stolen Generation case. The time we put in as teachers can have long-term impacts in sometimes unexpected ways.

Back to the Future

Eight years after leaving Clevo, I was back as the Aboriginal Studies teacher, my happy place. Despite the pay cut, it was a good move as I was teaching the children of students I had previously taught and so I had credibility in the community and therefore leverage with the students. The school was also half the size because of 'white flight' from the fallout of the devolution policy in the late 1980s and so the percentage of Aboriginal students was much higher. This created a close-knit, proactive staff who championed innovative strategies to meet the specific needs of the students. This included delivering Aboriginal Studies by distance education to a number of local high schools.

During this time, I had three children with my husband who is from the local Aboriginal community. I am more than proud of my kids who have grown up to be kind, caring and community-oriented people with one finishing her nursing degree, one working in logistics, and another working in a local Aboriginal organisation. They are proud of who they are and never forget where they come from. They love their sports and still play (and strap and coach) for Redfern All Blacks Football Club.

This time at Clevo was also where I first met Kylie (my inimitable co-author) in Year 10 and convinced her to stay on for Year 11. As honourable as my intentions sound when she speaks of this, I was also lobbying all the students to ensure we had enough students for a Year 11 class, but especially wanted students like Kylie who were hard-working, sincere and committed. Kylie, with all her health problems impacting her attendance, was one of the most hard-working and respectful students I had ever taught. She never gave up and persisted until she got through. Any teacher will tell you that when you get a student who is keen to learn, you never hesitate to put in the extra work to get them across the line. I never doubted that Kylie would go places, even though she sometimes seems surprised that she has.

Aunty Deb, who was and still is the AEO at the school, was (and still is) a critical mentor and support to me and other staff. She loves the kids and knows the families and communities and so her advice and guidance to working with the community is critical and appreciated. She is also amazing with the non-Aboriginal kids, including them in everything and creating a place of belonging for them as well.

When I was relieving Deputy and had to deal with discipline issues, Aunty Deb would be the one I sought advice from regarding the action to be taken, be that suspending a student and deciding whether to place them in in-school detention or sending them home. She always knew what would be best for the child and the family, which would allow us to solve issues before they blew up.

Because of this, we gained community trust with the more difficult issues and this became critical to the smooth running of the school. We also have a strong relationship outside of school being committed Souths and Redfern All Blacks supporters and having children and grandchildren of the same age. Many a footy or basketball game was attended together even though my kids and her grannies were often in different teams.

The Fight for Public Education

At the turn of last century, the Education Department decided to close this and other inner west schools due to falling student numbers. Their argument that families moving out of these areas meant that the schools were no longer viable was later proven short-sighted, especially given that at this time there was a development boom of medium-density housing. For the inner-city Redfern-Waterloo-Alexandria community this meant that there would be no secondary education in the area, and the nearest high school was two bus trips away. The plan was to close four small local primary schools, sell the land and move all the students into the Clevo site. While the local union took the fight to the government for all the affected schools, we took the fight to the Aboriginal community, and they didn't let us down.

Local community members, Aunties and Uncles, took the fight to the department by speaking at local public meetings to send the message that local Aboriginal children were going to be denied a secondary education in one of the wealthiest cities in Australia. Today, of course, the population graphs that were used to support the decision to close down schools have now reversed (as we suggested they would) as families move back to the city in droves. Now, not only is Alexandria Park Community School (once was Clevo and reconfigured into a K-12 school) one of the largest inner-city schools with the largest Aboriginal population in this area, another inner city high school has been built on the original Cleveland Street High School site to accommodate the growing population.

What I learned was the importance of standing up for your principles, finding allies and champions like local community member Uncle Terry, fighting for every child's right to education and the extra mile you must go to achieve this. I was also reminded of the significant relationships, connections and networks in my life that allowed me to do this work and how they will always shape the work that I do. On top of this, I learnt about the multifaceted nature of leadership and leading, especially leveraging, and strategising workarounds to achieve what might seem impossible.

The implementation of the new school was a bumpy ride with incomplete renovations, a principal who didn't understand the community, resistance from some primary teachers who were unhappy in a school with older kids and a few of our talented staff moving on. However, the K-12 school was embraced by the community as they could send all their children to the one place, reducing transition issues and creating possibilities for innovative curriculum and student support programs across the stages. Today, the school is going strong with a number of staff still there including the Aboriginal staff and a principal who embraces the community. This has resulted in a new building with local Aboriginal nomenclature, except the gym, which is named the Denzil in honour of Uncle Terry, long-time supporter and lobbyist for the school! I am lucky to still be involved in the school as a researcher and even though it has physically changed, it still feels like home.

My Final School

The last school I was in was another inner west secondary school with a high multicultural but low Aboriginal population and a range of students in selective, gifted and talented or local classes. There were a couple of staff members working on Aboriginal education initiatives including a compulsory Aboriginal languages subject in Year 7, but they struggled to find an Aboriginal community officer who would stay for long. I knew a local Aboriginal grandmother who was well respected in the community and had looked after my kids when I was at work or meetings and so I suggested her for the role. She instantly made a difference to the students and teachers alike. She was cluey and organised for the Aboriginal students to run the 'Big Morning Tea' annual fundraising event to raise money for breast cancer. While the kids got a lot out of this in terms of organisational skills, involving their own families and raising their profile in the school, the teachers were extremely impressed with the Aboriginal kids doing this work and so this significantly improved relationships within the school community.

I remember this one kid who had been difficult to engage with, and one day he was deliberately ignoring what he was supposed to be doing in class and drawing on a piece of paper. Coincidentally, another student asked what the word 'intricate' meant and, as I thought about the best way to explain it, I noticed that his drawing was in fact highly detailed and intricate, and so I used this to explain the word. I did this in a way that complimented his skill, as if he had drawn it specifically to help me teach the class. He was surprised, then lit up as many kids came over to look at his drawing, ask him how he did it, and if he could teach them to draw like that. Even though it distracted us from what the lesson was supposed to be about, I recognised it as a rare teachable moment and opportunity to get this kid on side, and it worked. Being that teacher that makes the difference, is being that teacher that gets out of the way and lets the kids roll with something that makes them feel good about themselves.

After two years at the school, I was asked to relieve in an Aboriginal centre at a local university for a year and was glad for the break after a hectic few years. I thoroughly enjoyed this work, lecturing in teacher education and organising professional experiences for Aboriginal students across the state, and so applied for and got a permanent position. I could see the value in sharing my teaching experiences with preservice teachers and perhaps giving them some tips so they were better prepared for teaching than I was. Despite the laborious work involved in getting a doctorate, I'm still there doing some interesting work around Aboriginal-led teacher professional learning and hoping to continue to positively influence teachers' lives and work.

Where I Am Now

I am still working at the university in Aboriginal education and teacher education, initially in writing and implementing compulsory units of study for all students and more recently, electives in Aboriginal Studies as a teaching area and courses that focus on Learning from Country (LFC) as a foundational philosophy for teaching. This also has a research component so that we can follow our graduates into their first few years of teaching to see if and how their university experiences have helped them. The results are better than we could have hoped for, with all teachers telling us about the different ways Learning from Country has impacted positively on their teaching regardless of their school context. LFC has helped them build relationships with students, whether they be Aboriginal, refugee, special needs or non-Aboriginal students. They feel confident in building relationships with Aboriginal staff and community, and this has also supported their teaching. Significantly, this conceptual approach is now a foundational and mandatory principle in the newly implemented (2022) Education Major and so all 500 or so students going through this degree each year will benefit from this approach. This will hopefully result in more teachers keen to make a difference for Aboriginal students, and indeed all students, in their school.

Finally, introducing the Master of Education: Leadership in Aboriginal Education is a joy as I get to work with passionate, committed and interesting Aboriginal and non-Aboriginal educators from across the country. I learn so much from them and could listen to their yarns about their schools, kids, colleagues and communities all day. Building these learning communities on a shared journey of making a difference is why I turn up every day.

Lessons I've Learnt

So, what has 40 years taught me?

- Relationships, relationships, relationships … at all levels and between all people on a daily basis.

- Demonstrating respect and trust with students, families, and communities to build the relationships necessary to make a difference.

- Understanding and leveraging the everyday significance of culture, identity and history and the interaction of these in power plays.

- Focussing on student strengths and building on these in and out of the classroom.

- Choosing the right person for the job and trusting, supporting, and encouraging them to do their best work.

- Leading by doing - don't expect your colleagues to do anything you wouldn't do yourself. Leading from behind and in the shadows is still leading.

- Different responses for different contexts and events, but always following your principles and values.

- Leverage your strengths to work on your shortcomings and surround yourself with people who get you. Stay clear of those who will try to undermine you – there will always be someone.

- Never accept defeat, always find workarounds to get the important things done – there's more than one way to skin a cat as my mother would say.

- Learning from Country and listening to Aboriginal voices is the key to education for all teachers and students, and to disrupting intergenerational cycles of trauma, disadvantage, and racism.

- Build learning communities where you can confidentially share wins, losses, ideas, hopes and dreams.

- Bask in the joy of the little wins that make a difference and keep you going.

END OF CHAPTER REFLECTION

What are three things you've learnt from Cathie's experience?

_____

_____

_____

_____

What are some key themes that stood out for you in this chapter?

_____

_____

_____

_____

_____

_____

Outline the key events in your career and what they have taught you along the way.

_____

_____

_____

_____

_____

_____

_____

_____

_____

_____

_____

_____

_____

_____

Chapter Three

THE LITTLE THINGS THAT MAKE A DIFFERENCE

In this chapter, we share little things that may support you with getting back to the basics of teaching and hopefully inspiring you to have a bit more fun with the process along the way. Everyone will have their own little tips and tricks and this is simply a light-hearted chapter to remind you of some of the things we often overlook or perhaps, due to the busyness of life and teaching, you've forgotten.

James Comer said, "No significant learning occurs without a significant relationship". We know this – the great Rita Pearson talks about the significance of relationships. If you're lacking motivation or direction as a teacher, it's uplifting to go back and watch Rita's TEDTalk. She will remind you why every child deserves a champion and highlight the fact that no significant learning can occur without a significant relationship. She'll leave you uplifted and inspired to do more and go deeper when it comes to teaching.

Relationships connect us with learning. Take a moment to think about professional learning courses you've been to. Is it the content or the facilitator you remember most?

If the facilitator takes the time to connect through yarning, humour and unpacking the 'why', you're more likely to engage, remember and put the content into practice.

The Power of Story Sharing

Simple strategies such as starting every lesson with a yarn and connecting the lesson to a real-life scenario or how it could benefit students in the future is a powerful engagement tool. There is a yarn that can be told about every lesson. If you can't find the why, go and ask questions and then come back to students with this information. Disconnected facts won't have a lasting impact on students. We need to teach with passion and purpose. Remember this when programming. Ask yourself, *why is this important?*

Find and create links before you start to teach it. Think about links that will not only support the students in their future ambitions, but also their family and wider community. Everyone loves to help and be of service to others. Sometimes students will give it a go if it will benefit others. By sharing stories, students begin to engage and light up because they connect the learning to a real-life scenario.

Knowing Your Students

Really getting to know your students and finding out what they like, dislike, what triggers them and what really engages them is a game-changer. You could create a little journal with pictures of your students and note down the things you learn about them throughout the year. This could be a great way to really start to notice those students who are slipping through the cracks, the ones who show up because they have to and who try their best to go unnoticed. Teachers that make a difference notice these kids and ensure they see them and do everything they can to bring the best out of them.

The Power of Fun and Bringing Joy to Learning

As educators, we must have fun with the creative process. We need to develop fun and engaging ways to ensure that our lessons will be absorbed. A simple engagement strategy that often helps is to allow students to take part in the planning. This ensures they feel valued and smart, and a part of the entire learning process. This is a difficult concept to comprehend as most of the planning is done during the holidays when society thinks teachers are out enjoying their 12 weeks off during the year. We know that many of those weeks are devoted to preparing rich and engaging lessons for students.

You could come up with the structure of the lessons and share your creative ideas with the class. By asking for their input, you really are demonstrating that you value student voice, and let's face it, kids are so creative and can find joy in anything. Allow them to support their learning and development. Give it a go and let us know what you think!

Keep It Strength-Based

That teacher who makes a difference focuses on the strengths. They see the things students don't and they go out of their way to help students see how deadly they really are.

When giving feedback to students, always start with the positives and guide the conversation to allow the student to reflect on where they think they could improve. Through a positive relationship, in those times where the conversation or feedback is tough, it'll be far better received if a relationship is established.

Our most challenging students really need your love, care and compassion.

Listen… Really Listen

Be sure to open your mind to learning and understanding other perspectives and actively demonstrate this through the act of deep listening. Despite teachers having an abundance of knowledge and expertise, there is so much to learn from the many creative minds that sit within your classrooms.

Listening is a skill and takes practice and commitment. Often when we engage in conversations or obtain new knowledge, our minds are accustomed to drafting up our response or our viewpoint without waiting for the person to finish. Pay attention to what's going on in your own mind and if you see yourself jumping in too soon with your thoughts or opinions, simply remind yourself to listen and listen deeply. Remember, sitting in your classrooms are some of the future change makers of the world. Take the time to learn from their knowledge and allow them the opportunity to flourish in your safe and supportive environment.

Be Adaptable to Change

Understanding that learning doesn't always go to plan and that your school may change direction, resources, leadership and many other things throughout your career, helps you adapt to change, especially unexpected change. Some may dig their heels in and fight against these changes - fighting is good at times, however there will be many times where you'll need to make the wise decision and choose where best to focus your energy. Pick your battles and the hill you are prepared to die on. Change is often good. It keeps us on our toes and in the mode of truly being lifelong learners.

Engage in Meaningful Collaboration

Why work alone when you can do it with others? We hear teachers who don't feel supported and are spending their weekends planning alone. Focus on the strengths within your team, build relationships within your school or community of schools and freely give and ask questions. Never be afraid to admit what you don't know and draw on the strengths of others. Leaders, which you are regardless of the title at school, allow themselves to be vulnerable and courageous. Lead by example and freely give of your knowledge and resources, and you'll find it shall be returned to you.

Be Engaging and Passionate

Your energy and passion is evident in how you go about your work. If you don't love or value what you're teaching, your students will quickly pick up on it. Rita Pierson says that teachers become great actors and actresses, so put on your best show and get into the topic. Smile and enjoy the process of learning. There is nothing worse than sitting through learning if the presenter is not enthusiastic or engaging. You can do it! Crank up your engagement surrounding the topics you teach and show the kids you're excited. Passion and enthusiasm is contagious - it will rub off on the kids.

Make Every Student Feel Important

Great teachers have a way to make every student feel important. They make them feel valued and cared for. They believe in students and instil a love of learning. Those who don't have a connection with a teacher often become disengaged or display behaviour problems. If they feel loved and cared for, they naturally want to reciprocate and show gratitude and kindness to their teacher. By valuing and believing in students, many students go on to have greater confidence, develop a growth mindset and will often begin to take risks in their learning.

Harness the Power of Feedback

Feedback has a way of either making or breaking a student. Once relationships are formed, teachers can provide constructive feedback to allow for areas of growth or development. It's important that feedback is always strength-based. There has to be a positive in every situation. If the student had a go, that's a great place to start. Verbal feedback is very important. If you're marking student work and providing written comments, be sure to let them know in a few words that you acknowledge their efforts and highlight some great points. A strategy may be to start with the positives, add in a few areas of improvement then end with a positive.

Know Your Community

You could be the most incredible teacher in the school community you're working in, but this does not necessarily mean you will have the same success if you were to move onto a new community. When working with Aboriginal families and communities, it takes time to develop the trust to get 'buy in'. As each community is different, it is important to learn as much as you can about your new school community before you get there. You can use the skills and experiences you have gained along the way, but when you get there, be a humble listener and learner.

When building relationships with Aboriginal families, we must remember that past policies and the mistreatment of Aboriginal peoples across the country have severed the trust in many government and educational systems. Many Aboriginal peoples were denied an education simply because they were Aboriginal. It was because of this trauma that many Aboriginal families still fear entering the school gates to discuss their child's education.

Trust and relationships take time to develop. As educators, it's important that you continue to show up to work on those relationships. Sometimes stepping outside the school gates and participating in community events is a great way to break down the barriers and allow yourself to be seen as a person wanting to make a difference and not as the authority figure parents often see you as at school.

When connecting with communities, we must always remember that Australia is an extremely diverse country with many language groups, clans and nations and therefore the stories and experiences from each group are different.

Learn, Un-Learn or Re-Learn

Prior to 1788, there were more than 500 Aboriginal nations in Australia; those nations have been here for at least 65,000 years. Within these nations there are communities and families who still maintain their connection to Country and culture. Aboriginal culture is not a thing of the past; the culture is alive and real. To successfully build relationships with our families, educators need to think creatively and innovatively about ways to invite families into the learning environment.

Educational systems and schools that listen to and respect the voices of the community really make a difference. Schools can be a place of healing and contribute to taking those first steps in achieving true reconciliation. It's important to recognise Australian history and to acknowledge the sadness that invasion brought upon the many nations and communities across the country.

It's important for Aboriginal communities for our history to be acknowledged because many feel that our history, tens and thousands of years of culture, have been swept under the rug.

Each clan and language group has their own beliefs, language, customs, Dreaming, and creation stories, and their own laws and lores.

We believe, however, that through education that listens to and respects the voices and stories of Aboriginal communities, we can come to a place of healing and perhaps, true reconciliation.

We must always remember that Australia is still a very new country and that the policies that have been implemented across the country have been discriminatory and created horrific circumstances and experiences for Aboriginal people.

Misunderstandings, Misinformation and Misconceptions

Conflict between schools, communities, teachers and families can be based on a misunderstanding often stemming from misinformation. This can occur as we as teachers often forget that we use a lot of jargon when we speak about our work and our students. For instance, we talk about our syllabus outcomes, units of work, evidence-based strategies etc. to describe and discuss our work, but these words can be meaningless to many outside of education, including parents and community. This can alienate and undermine parent agency when talking to teachers and principals.

Consequently, issues and tensions can escalate unnecessarily as teachers and parents are literally communicating in different languages. It is incumbent upon us to inform parents about the language we use or find different ways to make ourselves clear about what we mean when talking about education in relation to their children. This will also support parents in advocating for their children and us in understanding their concerns, and for all of us to come together to find the best solution.

Common Fears

Many teachers report not feeling confident in engaging with Aboriginal families or teaching Aboriginal content out of fear. Fear of offending and fear of getting it wrong.

Acknowledging the intergenerational trauma of past policies and mistreatment of Aboriginal families and communities, as well as providing a framework and support structure, can be a great way to begin the healing and reconciliation journey.

It's important to remember this when working with Aboriginal students and families. Even though they may not have been directly affected by trauma or discriminatory practices, research shows that the intergenerational trauma still affects them. They carry the sad stories and knowledge of past policies and systematic racism that have affected their parents and grandparents. Some Aboriginal families don't trust schools, government organisations or the people who work in them.

From our experience, most families and community members say that they want you to have a go. Respectfully learn and ask questions. Be honest in your teaching and learning and apologise if you get it wrong. Ask for help or advice and implement it when you try again.

Create Culturally Safe Learning Environments

To connect with families and communities, creating a culturally inviting safe space is paramount. Little things such as flying the Aboriginal and Torres Strait Islander flags is a sign that Aboriginal culture and heritage is respected and valued at the school. Acknowledging and adhering to protocols such as liaising with and connecting with appropriate Elders or community leaders and organisations is a good place to start when building authentic relationships with families.

Welcome and Acknowledgement of Country

Creating a localised acknowledgement of Country for the school sometimes brings great joy to local families, especially when they are invited to participate and contribute to the process. A Welcome and Acknowledgement of Country is a practice that is valued and respected across Australia. It's important to understand the difference between a Welcome and an Acknowledgement.

A Welcome to Country is generally conducted by a Traditional Owner or Custodian of the Country you're on. It's usually done by an Elder or respected community member, however, at times children and students do them if given the appropriate permissions. It's important to understand your local community and their protocols and adhere to these.

An Acknowledgement of Country can be done by anyone. It is a sign of respect that you acknowledge the traditional owners or custodians of the land and that you pay respect to the Country, Elders and the ancestors of that land for allowing you to live, work or visit the land you're on. A localised Acknowledgement of Country helps build relationships with the community as it demonstrates that their culture and history is respected.

Many schools have used this process to get to know their local community and invite Aboriginal Elders and community members into their school to work on a local Acknowledgement of Country. Some schools have also displayed these at the front of the school or on their noticeboard to demonstrate their respect and show the wider community that they acknowledge and respect Country.

Highlight Deadly Role Models Within Community

There are many deadly people within our communities who are doing incredible work and are making a difference. The sad truth is that the media have focussed their energy on the things that portray Aboriginal people in a negative light or the sporting stars or musicians - the select few who manage to make it through and become noticed for their talents. Students need to see what they aspire to be so it's crucial that you understand that Aboriginal students have many talents and interests. They may wish to become a tradesperson, business owner, teacher, lawyer, doctor or scientist. You'll be surprised how many incredibly talented Aboriginal people there are. Celebrate their success and highlight their deadly work to all students.

A Few Little Tips to Get Started

There are many books and resources you can use to learn how to respectfully connect with Aboriginal families. Simple things you can do is to fly Aboriginal and Torres Strait Islander flags, develop a localised acknowledgement of Country, and consult with Aboriginal students and families about important events initiatives at the school.

Send home positive letters, certificates or call home to share positive experiences, value the knowledge, time and experience of guests and offer a gift or remuneration as a token of appreciation for their time and knowledge. When you have Aboriginal families and community members visit the school, always put on a feed - from a simple cuppa and bikkies to a barbeque if the occasion calls for it. Having a yarn over a feed is often the best way to connect and if you're lucky an Aunty will bring some damper or johnny cakes from home. Food is a great way to connect and baking bread spans across all cultures.

END OF CHAPTER REFLECTION

List three strategies described in this chapter that you think you need to develop.

_____

_____

_____

_____

Identify a deadly community role model and describe how you might involve them in your classroom.

_____

_____

_____

_____

_____

_____

Write your own personalised Acknowledgement to Country.

Chapter Four

TEACHER WELLBEING MAKES A DIFFERENCE

To be that teacher who makes a difference, it's important to take care of yourself first in order to have the energy and passion to teach with enthusiasm and truly support students to their full potential.

Teaching has always been an incredibly difficult job, one that is underestimated by many. The time, passion and energy required from teachers can be overwhelming and draining. Recent reports state that the teacher shortage is growing daily due to many amazing teachers leaving the profession as a result of the stress of the job and the impact it has on their well-being.

In this chapter, we share tips on teacher wellbeing and how to ensure you look after yourself and create a sustainable work-life balance so that you can be the best teacher that you can be.

It's important to have a set timeframe and guidelines around when you work and allow a separation between work and home. We know that teaching is not a nine-to-three job as many assume. To truly value your worth in energy it's important you set up boundaries in regards to when and how much time you give to the profession. Whilst this book is about being that teacher that makes a difference, we know that you can't make a difference if you don't take care of yourself first.

Plan out your week. Update your calendar or diary with set times that you're going to work. Without a balance or clear outline about when is work time and when is family, home or 'me' time, it's easy to get caught up in a never-ending cycle of what always feels like work. To take care of our wellbeing, we all need to try our best to plan and remain in control of our work/life balance - easier said than done, we know!

Allocate the amount of time you are going to set aside in the evening and commit to that time. A strategy that you could use is to set a timer so that whatever you don't get done in that hour or time allocated, goes into the next lot of work allocated time.

Put an out of office message on your email stating your work hours and that any emails received outside of these hours will be dealt with during the next available workday. It is amazing how the volume of emails starts to decrease when you do this regularly. It also reduces unreasonable expectations that you will answer emails immediately.

Think about turning off phone notifications for your emails, social media and anything else that might cause you stress or make you feel like you have to keep working outside of work hours. If every time you pick up your phone, there are 20 email notifications, it is hard not to quickly check to see if there is anything urgent. Before you know it, you have spent a couple of hours answering emails in your own time. Ironically, the more efficient you are at responding to emails, the more people will expect you to answer them immediately.

If you need to work on the weekend, then allocate the time beforehand and make sure you stick to the allocated time. You may set aside an hour or so on a Sunday afternoon. We know teachers are creative and like to be productive because you want to do right by your students. However, you need to be disciplined and listen to your voice, know your body and know your mind so that you can best look after you.

Have a Teacher Wellbeing Buddy

In all workplaces, it's important to have a person who can keep you sane when times get tough. Someone who really knows you, what you're about and can be there as a sounding board to vent to and share ideas with, is extremely important.

Find a person who you can be real with. If you're not the greatest at art in a primary school setting, find a buddy who is great at and loves art and ask for their help and expertise. Don't ever be embarrassed about not knowing it all. There is a misconception that teachers need to know it all and feel like they have the skills and drive to work things out as they go.

Engaging with teachers who specialise in the things you are not great at is the smart thing to do, and you will have skills that you can share with them.

Put YOU first

Doing your absolute best doesn't mean working yourself into the ground and giving every bit of yourself to make a difference. You must always remember that you can't look after anybody else unless you take care of YOU first.

Every educator has the ability to multitask and is also very good at being an incredible actor or actress. They often cruise along with a smile on their face, getting all of the jobs done but inside they're slowly falling apart. Teacher and staff wellbeing should be at the forefront of every education setting, however, it's up to you as an individual to look after yourself and become a leader and encourage others to take care of themselves. There should be a reciprocal bond of collaboration and connection among teachers. It could be a good idea to start a teacher wellbeing group or committee to ensure that your school truly does value and demonstrate the importance of self-care, and relationships with staff and the school community.

Allow yourself a weekend free of schoolwork whenever you can. The good old saying "if you fail to plan you plan to fail" is important to remember as teachers. Plan for rest and wellbeing time.

It's reported that teachers experience as much stress as paramedics and police officers. High numbers of teachers are experiencing burnout. Many utilise unhealthy and damaging strategies to deal with work-related stress. Some of these include using drugs, alcohol or prescription medication.

The energy teachers bring to the profession is transferred to students. If a teacher is experiencing burnout or stress, that stress is brought into the classroom and those students will also experience high levels of stress and lower engagement in the classroom, which will ultimately lead to lower student performance.

Mindfulness and journaling are incredible ways for any individual to de-stress and focus on what they can do. It's important to always lead and teach from a place of passion and purpose. Without purpose or a vision about what we want to achieve, it's unlikely we'll achieve much success in our careers.

Regardless of what your career ambitions are within a school environment, it's important to set goals and ensure we as educators are continuously improving. We expect our students to grow and improve every year, so we should set those same expectations upon ourselves.

Start Your Day Right

Starting your day right can lead to a tremendous amount of productivity and enjoyment to your day. Below is a list of things you may wish to consider or trail for a period of time.

Journaling - There is something therapeutic and calming about journaling. It can support your wellbeing and lead to transformational change. Journaling can help prioritise your tasks, ideas and dreams. Start by writing your thoughts or goals, both long-term and short-term, along with things you're grateful for personally and professionally. It's like having a friend or mentor who is just there to listen without judgement. It's nice to look back and reflect on how far you've come.

Exercise - The importance of exercise to support wellbeing wouldn't be new to you, but a nice reminder for all of us. Many relate exercising to weight loss or looking a certain way, however the important thing we should associate exercise with is wellbeing and supporting mental health. No gyms are necessary, a simple 20 to 30-minute walk is enough to have you feeling accomplished, get the endorphins pumping, increase your energy levels and clear your head.

Meditating - There is tonnes of research to support the importance of meditation to bring a sense of calm, and overall improved health and wellbeing. Meditation doesn't need to be attached to spiritual practice; it can simply be the process of slowing down to give your mind the well-deserved break it deserves. There are many apps you can download to guide you through meditation or you could simply find a quiet place in your home to practise this incredible practice that many swear by.

Kylie refers to the above three wellbeing ideas as her JEM morning (Journaling - Exercise - Meditation) and recommends allocating even ten minutes towards each first thing in the morning. Housework, schoolwork and everything else on your to-do list can come after. What you'll find is that you'll most likely feel happier and more in control of your day ahead.

Visualisation - This is a powerful tool to use to attract or bring to fruition your greatest hopes and desires. Look up the law of attraction or visualisation and you'll find that many of the world's successful people use the power of visualisation, from entrepreneurs to change agents to elite athletes.

Student Strengths and Gratitude Journal

Teaching is a tough job and it's easy to get caught up in the ongoing pressures of achieving improved outcomes and gathering evidence and data to support your work. During tough times, it's important to bring your focus back to the 'why' and the things that matter most - your students. You may wish to try using a student strengths and gratitude journal, which is basically a book with student photos and a section for you to note their strengths and all the little things you're grateful for. It could be a nice compliment or card they gave you, or a kind gesture you witnessed. When you see these things, note them down and from time to time, glance back and smile with pride and gratitude for the opportunity to support their journey. Hopefully, this exercise will help you to find more joy in your profession and remind you of the important role you have in changing lives and shaping your students into wonderful humans.

END OF CHAPTER REFLECTION

What are three things you do to improve to support your wellbeing and have a better work/life balance?

_____

_____

_____

_____

What is a creative way to bring more joy into the workplace?

_____

_____

_____

_____

_____

Fast forward to the end of your career and write a letter reflecting on the wonderful career you've had, focussing on the difference you've made in the lives of countless students.

_____

_____

_____

_____

_____

_____

_____

_____

_____

_____

_____

_____

_____

_____

_____

Be That Teacher Who Makes A Difference

Chapter Five

DEEP LISTENING MAKES A DIFFERENCE

How do we become that teacher who makes a difference, particularly for our Aboriginal students who sometimes struggle in our classrooms? We can find out more about our students' histories and cultures by collaborating with their families and communities to learn from Country. Listening to Aboriginal community members has an enormous impact on the way in which we are seen as teachers, and the way students see us as learners. Understanding the impact of colonisation and the importance of Aboriginal voices is a great place to start. Experiencing Country as teacher, exploring the type of teacher we want to be and how we want to make a difference for our students are important considerations.

On realising the impact of this approach, at university we teach Aboriginal community engagement courses for preservice teachers to participate in Learning from Country activities. Here, they go out onto local Country (Gadigal land) and listen to local Aboriginal narratives of place - histories, cultures and lived experiences. This is a transformative experience for many, and so the 2022 cohort have generously agreed to share their responses to these experiences to inspire teachers to take this journey.

One of the important lessons is how to reflect on your cultural background and what this means in relation to learning from Country. Here, preservice teachers reflect deeply on their experiences of learning from Country and the power of listening to Aboriginal voices and write about, record and/or visually represent these experiences in the form of a blogpost, podcast, visual learning diary or photo story. Their reflections below reveal their 'lightbulb' moments that have prompted deep thought about what it means to be an educator. Key messages here are the importance of connecting with Aboriginal students, their families, and communities, and shifting your thinking to focus on a 'Black Excellence' perspective instead of the negatives.

It was a disturbing yet eye-opening experience for me, forcing me to reflect on how I will connect with my students and their families when I start teaching.

Listening to Kylie made me reflect upon and be in awe of the power and strength of Aboriginal women and I am saddened by the abundance of knowledge that has been forcefully left untold. Invaders colonised this land and when they reached out to communicate with Aboriginal groups, they looked to men assuming they held positions of power.

Listening to a parent champion Blak Excellence was inspiring, as it encouraged me to reflect on how a shift in perspective can go a long way.

Deep listening to the lived experiences of trauma and tragedy deeply affected me and this prompted me to reflect on the intergenerational trauma that stemmed from colonisation. Indeed, the removal of children from their homes affected Indigenous peoples' cultural, spiritual, and family ties and thus continues to affect their wellbeing in medical, spiritual, and psychological ways.

This prompted me to reflect on how the Learning from Country Framework entails a pedagogical shift by connecting to Country through truth-telling. This is articulated through Aboriginal people sharing their knowledge of local contexts and on Country rather than in the classroom.

As an educator, this experience allowed me to reflect on my understanding of intergenerational trauma and how it might surface in my classroom. I realise I need to be there to listen, understand and support Aboriginal students to find resources to help overcome the trauma and improve well-being.

The haunting stories shared by victims of the Kinchela Boys Home atrocities was a real moment of deep reflection for me, and I think fired up a real call for action from every student in that room.

I reflected on how we can become caught up in focussing on the negatives, such as the inequity faced by Aboriginal people, and can forget to also focus on positives and celebrate the achievements of Aboriginal people. Celebrating Aboriginal children's achievements is important to supporting their development, self-esteem, and sense of belonging. This sense of belonging, as well as trust and mutual respect, is key to building positive community relationships and supporting Aboriginal children.

Listening to Aboriginal Voices

We all like listening to local Aboriginal voices and yarning to find out more about each other. Elders, knowledge holders, family workers, curators, youth workers, Stolen Generations and their descendants, political activists and educators told yarns about their lived experiences as an Aboriginal person in this country. Every speaker is closely connected to this community as well as having strong ties to their own Country which is often somewhere else. This gathering of like-minded advocates is embedded in place and at the same time significantly influences and changes place. It is important to listen to diverse voices so that you get a better understanding of the complexities of Country and communities to think critically about how this impacts on your role as a local teacher. This prompts reflection, humility, and an openness to engage with Aboriginal families and communities and build these relationships.

Indeed, the act of deep listening to Aboriginal community voices positions truth-telling as essential to challenging deficit discourses about Aboriginal and Torres Strait Islander people. Therefore, it is crucial to provide opportunities where students can appreciate the depth and longevity of Indigenous knowledge.

Through hearing the Stolen Generation survivors speak I felt a deep connection and emotion. One thing that will stick with me was that Uncle kept thanking us for listening, which showed how sharing his story, even though it was painful, was also healing.

Those shared traumatic experiences, opened my eyes to the brutal, recent history of our nation – and the effects of this trauma on the community. Hearing about it in history is not the same as listening to the stories. That was a very heavy class.

We also heard from one of the parents who really emphasised the importance of recognising Blak Excellence within the community. I found this really important because if you focus on just the challenges, it's easy to forget about everything that Aboriginal people do that is excellent. It is clear that there is a strong sense of pride and boldness within the Aboriginal community, and this is something that we should really be pushing. If people see a version of who they can become it's really motivating, and I think that's really great for the youth of our communities.

Learning From Country

Experiencing Country as a teacher heightens our awareness and sensitivity to the place on which we are learning. This sense of place and belonging is tactile, emotional, and eye-opening – as one preservice teacher noted, '*I began to feel more connected to the land I was walking on*'. Slowly the preservice teachers were experiencing everyday places differently, seeing new possibilities for teachable moments that could also change the way their students would experience their place. Country therefore has a role in educating us all.

Uncle's knowledge of ecologies and medicine was a powerful and transformative learning experience which allowed me to appreciate the intricate knowledge systems of Indigenous people and their scientifically accurate understanding of both Country and body and the ways they are connected.

Something that really struck me was how connected I felt to the things we were learning about. Being on Country made me feel curious and showed me that experiential learning can have that effect on students.

This component of the unit solidified non-verbal, non-linear and story sharing elements of Indigenous pedagogy. The accounts were harrowing and eye-opening; it really underlined how story sharing is so impactful, and it is such a relevant and impactful medium for learning from Country and learning in general.

The knowledge Uncle carries about the local Country was pretty mind-blowing, and it was so interesting to hear about the traditional uses and healing properties of so much flora that I've so casually passed by previously, without so much as a thought other than admiring their beauty.

Learning from Country in the city is a great way, I believe, to show students that Aboriginal culture is not the stereotypical representations they see in textbooks or on TV, but that it exists vibrantly amongst the concrete walls of cityscapes too.

The Type of Teacher I Want to Be

Overwhelmingly, we relate our learning from Country experiences to our role as a teacher of the next generation of Aboriginal children and all children, and what that means for the type of teacher we want to be. The preservice teachers expressed a responsibility as an educator to understand, respect, share and support students and their families, in an effort to challenge and change the status quo that marginalises Aboriginal students. They draw inspiration from Aboriginal advocates and activists and hope that they too can be agents of change.

Kylie shared her experience about how schools and educators can embrace Aboriginal ways of understanding, sharing knowledge and valuing to support the success of Aboriginal students. She shared practical ways in which educators can privilege Aboriginal ways of learning, e.g. yarning, storytelling, local protocols and symbols, outdoor experiences on Country, and inviting parents and community members to share their knowledge with students (rather than appropriating it).

Uncle spoke with so much passion that he had you really understanding how much of a responsibility we as white Australians have to put in the work of knowing this information, in order to be culturally responsive teachers in our classrooms.

As a future teacher, I aim to create learning experiences which challenge negative stereotypes of Aboriginal and Torres Strait Islander people and thus promote respectful and appreciative values of Indigenous culture amongst all students.

From a teaching standpoint, this really helped me see all the different ways that we can incorporate Aboriginal knowledges throughout the curriculum and get students to respect the wealth of First Nations knowledges.

This gave me a whole new perspective on how to engage with students in the future because I now understand that what I thought was the best call of action may not be. I always need to consider the children first and try to have empathy and really gain an understanding of what that family might be going through, and the adversities they might have to overcome to even get their child to school on that particular day.

I found this experience to be incredibly moving, confronting, informative, and inspiring, in both listening to Aunty speak of her experiences, and seeing the incredible space she has built for local families. Her determination and dedication towards making her students and families feel loved, nurtured, and reminding them that they have a safe space to come to, really left me in pure admiration and has given me so much inspiration for ways I can connect with Aboriginal students in my classroom.

How I Want to Make a Difference

Finally, these experiences motivate us to make a difference as we draw strength from Aboriginal educators to challenge ourselves, be brave and make change. Preservice teachers drew on the Aboriginal speakers' passion and commitment to break generations of oppression, marginalisation and intergenerational trauma that has hindered Aboriginal success. Again, the significance of relationships, connections and belonging is reinforced, leaving an indelible impression on preservice teachers who themselves vow to make a difference in the lives of their students.

Kylie helped ease my fear of offending Aboriginal people by reassuring us that Aboriginal communities will see the effort we are putting in rather than the mistakes. On reflection, I now know that I personally do not have to be an expert but rather a passionate, culturally responsive educator who supports positive change.

The Aboriginal community worker told us that Aboriginal peoples' distrust in schooling institutions can come from generations of mistreatment. It's my role to build this trust with students by creating a respectful classroom that is a safe space to build genuine relationships with students.

The emotion and pain in the room was palpable, but in hearing those stories and bringing them to light, I felt as a room it was a shared feeling of motivation as educators to do what we could in our roles to support breaking those cycles of intergenerational trauma. As an educator I want to hold onto the grief that I felt in that room for the people that were and still affected by those policies and use it to motivate and inform my actions.

Kylie reinforced the importance of protocols, cross-cultural understanding, and communication skills, demonstrating genuine interest, and acknowledging Country. She also impressed upon us the importance of education as a tool for effecting a better and more culturally responsive Australia, that hefty vital task on the shoulders of anyone who considers themselves just, including teachers. She inspired me to not be afraid of teaching Aboriginal knowledges, but rather to just give it a go and know I am helping to decolonise Australia.

I aim to embrace Aunty's sentiment in my classroom to build strong and genuine relationships with local Aboriginal families and broader communities so as to respect Australia's whole history and give my students meaningful learning experiences.

The Future is Bright

Seeing how these preservice teachers embraced the learning from Country experiences and reflected on these in relation to their future role as a teacher, is simultaneously humbling and exciting. Their level of psychological, cultural, and emotional commitment suggests that they too will engage their students in place-based learning on Country so the next generation of Australians will grow up with a deep level of knowledge, understanding and appreciation of Aboriginal contributions to Australian society. This gives us hope for the future of the teaching profession and education more broadly.

We hope that teachers will be inspired to start learning from Country where they live and work and think about how they can use this to build better classrooms.

END OF CHAPTER REFLECTION

What are three key takeaways from these preservice teachers' experiences?

_____

_____

_____

_____

Think about how you might implement Aboriginal-led professional learning for your staff.

Start by identifying possible experiences in your community and who could deliver these.

_____

_____

_____

_____

Next, consider how you would 'sell' this idea to the executive team and staff - list three possible strategies to do this.

_____

_____

_____

_____

Finally, identify three ways this PL could have an impact in the classroom.

_____

_____

_____

_____

_____

Chapter Six

CATHIE'S TIPS FOR DEADLY TEACHING

Classroom management relies on a few key understandings:

- students want and need clear structure, boundaries, and expectations.

- implement a small set of simple, effective routines from day one and maintain these throughout the year.

- persevere and be consistent - as a close friend used to say, it's either me or them, and it's not going to be me!

- recognise when something is not working and be prepared to change, even if it means temporarily losing face. Hopefully, you can make it a win for them without it being a loss for you.

- solve behavioural issues yourself - only escalate to the next level as a last resort. Kids need to see you in charge and able to solve problems fairly and efficiently to gain their confidence.

- remember that every student is someone's son or daughter and think about how you want people to treat your children. In saying that, consequences must be impartially applied for unacceptable behaviour.

- have some simple techniques that are either a reward or consequence and use these wisely.

- know your kids and what techniques work best for each one.

Clear and Consistent Routines

It is important to keep routines simple, clear, and consistent. The hard work is at the beginning of the year when you are setting these up. Allow students to be involved in discussion about classroom rules and routines. Demonstrating a collaborative approach can flow to productive and motivational student learning habits. It can also promote enjoyment, inclusive and innovative class work while still maintaining student focus on the task at hand. The more engaging and inclusive your classroom, the more kids will learn.

Settling the Class

To settle a class, particularly after a break (and on a windy day), I would put notes on the board before they came in so they could start writing in their books as soon as they sat down. This gets their book and pen out without me having to nag them. Some would complain but they would usually settle pretty quickly and start writing the notes. I would use the time to walk around and see if anyone was still unsettled and 'encourage' them to get the notes down so they didn't get behind the rest of the class. I would also use this time to observe the disposition of the class as a whole. When I felt the class was settled, I would talk about what we were going to do for the rest of the lesson and start with something engaging to get them going. I didn't worry if the lesson wasn't finished when the bell rang. I felt it was more important to get them settled as learning is limited until they are ready to engage and focus.

These days, there is an abundance of transition resources available thanks to the evolving world of technology. Depending on grade and setting, many use guided meditations or other transitional programs. While all these different options are great, it is important to remember that consistency is king.

Move Around

It's important to be mobile and move around a lot in class, not just sit at the front. Sometimes, I'd move to the back of the class and the kids wouldn't always notice I was there, or they'd be unsure what I was doing. Sometimes, I'd be quiet and observe, other times I'd look at their books, or just start talking to the notes on the board and explain what we're doing and why. If I was looking at their books, I would always point out something good they had done. Add a couple of ticks, a sticker or a stamp, particularly if they lacked confidence in their work. Perhaps I'd start up a yarn about what's happening at school, or suggest what we might do for the fun part of the lesson - something that I knew that they really wanted to do.

A Deadly Seating Plan

Secondary teachers often have many classes, so you could have around 150 students every week. Remembering their names gets harder as you get older. When I had three Year 7 classes in the same year I decided to sit them all in alphabetical order to see if this would help. They had to line up outside the classroom in alphabetical order (it's surprising what a challenge that is, even for a selective class) and then had to sit in that order in class.

It is a good technique for implementing the classroom routine and has a built-in reward system by allowing them to move next to their friends if they are working quietly. Sitting with their friends is the endgame and I let them know that this was possible if they work hard and are quiet. They also understood that if this didn't work, they would return to alphabetical order. Without fail, top or bottom class, they were sitting with their friends before the end of the term.

A positive aspect of this was that every student had someone to sit next to, no-one was left out or ostracised and in Year 7, kids had a chance to make new friends from different primary schools. This was especially helpful for the selective class as most were the only students from their primary school and were nervous making new friends in high school.

Divide and Rule

This is a simple way to get kids to cooperate, but one you use sparingly, as it is not really something that necessarily engenders good relationships. However, it can be a quick and easy means to an end if needed. For instance, if the bell goes and the kids are restless, you don't let them go until everyone is settled. There is always one kid who won't be quiet, and letting the class know that they can't go to lunch until this student settles down puts the pressure on that student to be quiet. This takes the heat off you as the 'baddie' and works quickly as most kids don't want to get on the wrong side of a whole class. When the student is quiet you thank them and let the class go!

Minutes to Go

A simple technique to calm down the class is to place a '1' (for one minute) on the board when the students are noisy (and after a few warnings). This represents the amount of time you will keep them in if they don't settle down. They will ignore this until you put another '1' next to it (now two minutes). At this point, if they are not used to this, they will ask what is happening and you let them know this is how long the whole class is staying in for being noisy. After their howls of indignation when you add on another '1', you let them know that you can erase these if they settle down.

At this point, they either complain more which attracts another '1' or they start to quieten down and do their work. The trick is to rub off the last '1' you put on as soon as there is a noticeable change in the class so they see that it is possible to reverse the situation. Hopefully, the numbers will be rubbed off by lunch. Even if there is a couple left, two minutes is not long for you but seems like a long time for them. When they are used to the system, someone will usually notice after the first time you put up a '1' on the board and tell the rest of the class to be quiet so they can go to lunch.

Calming the Class

Speaking just loudly enough for students to hear can quieten everything down and is better than yelling. So many times, I see teachers yelling louder than the kids, who often see this as a game and elevate the noise level. I wonder how the teacher does not have a raging headache by the end of the day. Instead, I would calm the class by speaking quietly enough so that they had to quieten down to hear me. I might have had to throw in a couple of key words like 'lunch detention', but I found overall that this often brought the volume of the room down and allowed for a chance to reset and refocus.

Yarn to Connect

When I tried to establish a relationship with kids, I would find time in each lesson to have a yarn with a different student. To find out what their interests were, who their mob (family) is and where they're from (Country or suburb), I'd find a point of connection so I could continue the yarn in the playground or the next time I saw them. This not only helped me connect and better understand each student and where they're coming from, but also inspired some ideas for lessons, and how to incorporate their cultural knowledge and lived experiences into the curriculum so they could see their world reflected at school.

This information can also be revealed in carefully planned formative assessment tasks like reflective writing that encourages students to contribute their own ideas and experiences. Building this sense of belonging is critical to inclusive and dynamic learning environments.

Explicit Instructions

Being explicit in your directions as well as the information you are trying to get kids to understand is critical to their confidence and learning. Thinking through how to break down more complex concepts or skills into simple and achievable parts, works with all kids and can be structured so that they learn at their own pace and can accrue regular rewards along the way. This aspect of your program differentiation takes a bit of work to set up initially but once done, it can be used repeatedly and becomes easier and quicker the more you do it. If you create a standard set of steps or procedures that the kids become familiar with, then they will apply these steps themselves.

Being explicit is often critical for kids with literacy issues, English as a second language, who lack confidence or have missed a lot of school. This helps you as the teacher to identify where and how they struggle, and thus be more specific about how to help them. Patience and perseverance is important and for some students, you will need to give them time to ask questions away from the other students, or confidentially outside of class.

Essentialise, Visualise and Backward Mapping

I know teachers are under pressure to get through a lot of content, meet many outcomes and elicit extensive data from students. What I did to manage this was work out the essential concepts, information, and skills the kids really needed to know for the topic, get rid of the 'fluff' and simplify the content without compromising the integrity of key concepts.

I find that if I visualise the 'big idea' underpinning the topic to formulate the major assessment task and then work backwards from this, I can build student skills and understandings to reach this point. If you work in a collaborative faculty, planning can be shared and coordinated across all the classes. Except for the senior years where you need to largely teach for the exam (at least in NSW for the Higher School Certificate), you can adjust assessments to cater for all ability levels and make sure all kids feel valued, smart and successful.

In-School (Rather Than After-School) Detention

In my experience, giving kids detention after school is ineffective, time-consuming and because it's not immediate, has little impact. Instead, keeping a student in for five minutes at recess or lunch has an immediate impact and ensures that the kids know you are serious. Five minutes is generally all you need – five minutes to a kid in their lunchtime feels like a long time to them as they know they are missing out on their handball or touch footy game.

If you don't have them in class before the break, you need to be prepared to get them from the playground if they don't turn up. It's annoying and time-consuming but you often only need to do it a couple of times to let them know you are serious. When I did this, I would go to the playground and stand in the middle of their game until they came with me. This made them unpopular with their friends, which was often worse than being in detention. Of course, I would have tried several in-class tactics to avoid getting to this point, but if I did, then I ALWAYS followed through. If you don't, the kids won't take you seriously and you will have ongoing discipline problems. The time you put in early in the year certainly pays off later.

Parent Relationships

Here's why it's important to have a good relationship with parents. If you make connections and call or send positive notes home about their child when you can (these can be brief and about a simple achievement or improvement), then when you need to call home to discuss poor behaviour and lack of effort in class, the parents are more likely to be prepared to listen and support your efforts to improve their child's attitude. After all, I've never met a parent who doesn't want their kids to do well at school.

As a last resort and if nothing else has worked or the student continues to do the same thing over again, I'd tell them that I would ring home. Often, I found out that the parent was having similar issues with their child at home so I try to work with them to come up with some ideas that we both could use. If you have that relationship with the parent then they are more likely to be willing to work with you to reinforce the message at home. I would let the child and family know about even small improvements so that interactions became more positive and hopeful. It can be time-consuming, but often prevents worse outcomes such as suspension or truanting. I feel this is time well spent and the word soon gets out to other parents and children.

END OF CHAPTER REFLECTION

Think about the tips and tricks you use to maintain a calm and inclusive classroom. Write a 'how to' summary for an early career teacher or intern to help them settle into school. We often overlook the value of this tacit knowledge, and your words of wisdom could be a 'make or break' moment for this person!

Tip 1

_____

_____

_____

_____

Tip 2

_____

_____

_____

Tip 3

Chapter Seven

FEAR OF GETTING IT WRONG

Teachers sometimes struggle to implement authentic Aboriginal content into their programs that is not tokenistic, essentialised or offensive to Aboriginal people. This chapter identifies those barriers and offers some ideas about how to address these issues if and when they arise.

In the current context of increasing demands to teach everything from first aid to life skills, teachers can become overwhelmed by the number of outcomes in their syllabus, and the prescriptive way in which they are expected to teach them. This increases the depth, breadth and complexity of the content that needs differentiating, resourcing and continually updating to prepare students for a rapidly changing world. This pressure can limit time and capacity to include Aboriginal content especially if this is not explicit in the syllabus and supported by resources. As Aboriginal content is often not mandatory, it can be easier to leave out or make tokenistic gestures to it.

Lack of Knowledge

One of the key hurdles is a lack of knowledge often stemming from poor or no education in this area at school or university. Compounding this is the often negative, simple stereotypes and misinformation presented by the media geared towards prompting emotive and divisive responses such as blaming Aboriginal people for their own disadvantage. Without the knowledge or skills to counteract this, you can feel powerless to challenge your colleagues or students when the inevitable questions and complaints arise. Knowing where to start and how to guide and organise your own re-education can be tricky, time-consuming, and easily consigned to the too hard basket.

We believe that, as a teacher, you have a responsibility to yourself and your students to learn about key issues that impact on your students, as you would with any other subject area. To improve your understanding about a range of Aboriginal issues, there are several reliable internet sites that you can access. These are generally local, state and commonwealth government sources, institutions such as universities, statutory bodies such as the Human Rights Commission and non-government organisations (NGOs) such as Reconciliation Australia. Also tap into your local school and community resources. Aboriginal community members are often happy to help if you are a willing, respectful listener and learner.

Lack of Confidence

Many teachers we've had in our professional learning sessions hesitate because they don't want to offend Aboriginal people. They don't want to teach the wrong thing. It makes them nervous and a bit anxious. They're worried that if they do the wrong thing, they could cause more harm than good, or put their community or the Aboriginal kids offside and forever damage future relationships. So, teacher confidence is a big consideration when supporting the implementation of Aboriginal curriculum.

Actively finding out more about Aboriginal issues will increase confidence, especially if you start including your knowledge in classroom discussions. Find allies in colleagues, parents and community members and engage in challenging conversations to keep growing. They will be keen to develop their own knowledge as well as create a collective knowledge base that you can all share for teaching and learning. Pretty much what you expect of your students. Baby steps with lots of reinforcement. Celebrate the small achievements because these combine to make significant change.

Lack of Commitment or Relevance

Effective teaching in Aboriginal Education takes passion, commitment, and time. It's the long game and so it doesn't happen overnight. Unfortunately, some teachers don't see the relevance of Aboriginal content, particularly if they teach in a subject area where there isn't much information or direction about how to include this. For some, if there isn't clear reference to Aboriginal ideas or issues in the syllabus, then it is easier not to take the extra time to include it.

There is Aboriginal content in every syllabus, but it helps if you can think outside the box and be creative. Look at how it is included in similar subject areas and explore the key curriculum support resources such as the Australian Curriculum and state-based syllabuses. Use the Aboriginal and Torres Strait Islander Cross Curriculum Priority (CCP) to identify syllabus outcomes that could include Aboriginal content and then list syllabus outcomes that could be adapted. For example, a holistic approach to a particular issue is one way to think about an Aboriginal way of understanding a particular concept. Also think about pedagogical approaches – what is a teaching/learning strategy that reflects Aboriginal ways of doing, such as using yarning circles to discuss issues and brainstorm ideas.

I Don't Teach Aboriginal Students

Some teachers mistakenly believe that because they don't have Aboriginal students in their classroom, they don't need to include Aboriginal content. They think that the Aboriginal perspectives are only for Aboriginal children. However, it is important that all Australians learn about Aboriginal and Torres Strait Islander histories, cultures and communities if we are to move from deficit to strength-based narratives. We all know if you talk about children in a negative way they translate this to low expectations, and will meet those expectations. Research has shown (Ladwig et al., 2009) that if high quality assessment tasks are given to students, then they will perform at a higher level.

Until we have more people educated about the true history of Australia including the relationship between Aboriginal and non-Aboriginal people, Aboriginal people won't get justice and a sense of recourse for past wrongs, and we can't as a nation move towards a shared history, healing, and improved quality of life for all.

Aboriginal content is for ALL students because it's about the nation's story, of which the Aboriginal narrative is foundational and fundamental. All teachers are teachers of this history and so, if we want to understand ourselves as Australians, we need to understand our whole history, including our Aboriginal history. Smart and engaged students enjoy the challenge of tackling the complex, relational and holistic issues inherent in Aboriginal topics and questions.

The NSW Department of Education, Aboriginal Education Policy has been in place in NSW since 1982. It states that Aboriginal education is for all students and is everybody's business, thus all teachers are accountable for implementing this.

Superficial Content

It is said that Aboriginal content is 'bolted on' rather than 'built in' and so the implementation of syllabi and support materials can be minimal and/or tokenistic. This often leaves teachers concerned about how to implement authentic content with integrity. Often, Aboriginal perspectives are attached in a more 'ad hoc' fashion instead of a coherent narrative that teachers and students can understand and engage with.

This increases the burden for teachers who have to 'fill in the gaps' and find ways to draw these perspectives together into a substantial and sequential scope and sequence that honours Indigenous knowledges rather than dilutes or essentialises them. Simplistic and tokenistic content can do more harm than good, particularly to Aboriginal students who find themselves marginalised and often forced to justify their Aboriginality.

Build your curriculum narrative from a local place-based platform. Knowing what Country your school is on is the best start and then you will then be able to do an Acknowledgement of Country and discuss this with your students.

There's a good chance your school has already embraced this protocol. Moving beyond this means asking and learning from Aboriginal colleagues, families and community members about the local area including Aboriginal organisations. Work with your colleagues, Aboriginal staff and community to think about how to embed this more broadly across the whole curriculum in ways that continually build this narrative. Students love learning about their local area when it reflects their experiences and interests and is seen by the school as valuable knowledge.

Use Version 9 (2022) of the Aboriginal and Torres Strait Islander Cross Curriculum Priority to scope and sequence Aboriginal content across subjects, faculties, stages, and the whole school. This version offers a more in-depth and rigorous approach to each dimension, including better framing of important socio-cultural and political issues that continue to impact on Aboriginal lives. Utilise the Stage 4 & 5 Aboriginal Studies syllabus as this is constructed as modules on particular topic areas, such as Aboriginal oral and written expression (use in English, history), Aboriginal technologies and environments (use in technology, science, geography) etc. The core areas of Aboriginal Identity and Aboriginal Self-Determination and Autonomy are also important concepts that can be embedded in many curriculum areas.

'Gap' Talk and Racism

Unfortunately, deficit discourses about Aboriginal peoples, histories and cultures continue to seep through media, government and some textbooks and resources. The frequent reference to Aboriginal people as disadvantaged above all else positions them as inferior, unfortunate and weak, often prompting disdain, contempt and pity. This is used to justify coercive control of resources and undermines self-esteem, self-determination, and agency, as well as positioning the government as 'saviour'. Along with the prevalence of casual racism in the playground and staff room, teachers often struggle to know the best way to counteract this without alienating students and colleagues. Racism continues to be persistent, insidious and covert for Aboriginal students.

Recent research, such as the Australian Reconciliation Barometer survey (2020), confirms this and so it is often up to teachers and schools to call out and lead the way in addressing racism. Aboriginal parents and students often don't expect the school to believe and/or understand the impact of racism on their children and so will move their children to another school that deals with this more effectively. The double bind here is that the education system labels the family as transient, unreliable and therefore not interested in education. We have seen this repeatedly as teachers and parents of Aboriginal children, and it hasn't improved over time.

In fact, with the rise of social media and 'fake' news, being racist is seen as a right justified by freedom of speech, and a protest against 'political correctness' and 'woke' or 'cancel' culture. It doesn't help when this comes from the nation's leaders, for instance, when the former Attorney General George Brandis stated that Australians had *'a right to be bigots'*, in a statement of support for diluting racial hatred laws (see Soutphommasane, 2019, pp. 70–78).

As educators concerned with the wellbeing of all students, we are obligated to call out individuals and institutions that do harm through language, discourses and actions. At the school level, anti-racism needs to be built into policies, procedures and strategies, and schools that do this well are proactive in creating inclusive classrooms and structures. One way to counteract negative and harmful talk is to flip what is being said to a strength-based statement - use language such as Black Excellence and community leadership and keep reminding people that we live and work on unceded land, that we need to embark on truth-telling and treaty-making.

Use the Alice Springs (Mparntwe) Education Declaration (2019) to support your curriculum, pedagogy and community engagement choices in the face of criticism as it says the purpose of education is to create a 'a socially cohesive society that values, respects and appreciates different points of view and cultural, social linguistic, and religious diversity' (p. 4).

The more these messages are talked about, the more likely that they will happen.

Limitations of Teaching Standards

While the intent of the Australian Standards for Teaching is to help teachers understand and account for the work they do, for many, it adds another layer of administrative work. It also highlights the government view of teaching as technical rather than coming from a place of passion and purpose and therefore offers little in terms of tapping into the reasons why and how teachers make a difference in the lives of their students. Some say it fails to acknowledge or understand the ethical and moral imperatives that underpin the efforts of teachers and schools.

With only two standards directly referencing Aboriginal and Torres Strait Islander peoples and knowledges, much of what is taught by the committed, enthusiastic, and talented teacher implementing authentic Aboriginal curriculum is not represented in these standards. It's problematic that the Aboriginal standards are represented in only one of three domains - professional knowledge - and not in the professional practice or professional engagement domains, especially given governments' stated policy priority of engaging with Aboriginal communities.

As a teacher, you can assess all the teaching standards and identify where you can manipulate these to reflect the work you are doing in Aboriginal curriculum, pedagogy and community engagement. In particular, look at the professional practice and professional engagement dimensions and articulate the work you are doing in these contexts.

Surface Level Leadership

Leadership positions and the role of leadership is critical for improving Aboriginal student engagement and learning. It is important to note the difference between leadership and authority. Those in leadership positions may have the authority to make decisions and allocate resources but it doesn't necessarily make them leaders. True leaders don't need a position or authority to lead. They lead by creating the conditions and empowering others to lead.

Research across Australia (as reported by Trimmer et al., 2019) notes that schools where principals and leaders genuinely engage with the community in a 'both-ways' approach to leadership have better results than those who don't. Unfortunately, there is plenty of lip service leadership in schools where good visuals and the right words imply authentic engagement but on a closer look, are absent where more difficult structural and policy decisions are needed.

An example of this is when a teacher is keen to introduce an Aboriginal Studies elective and it is placed on the timetable against other popular subjects such as Art or Sport and so makes it difficult to get enough students to elect the course. Committed leadership will support the introduction of this subject, particularly if Aboriginal students are keen to do it. The inclusion of this subject in the curriculum sends an important message, as well signifying that the school takes seriously its moral and ethical obligation to address diversity and inclusion. In our experience, the introduction of Aboriginal Studies as a subject in its own right provides a platform for change across the curriculum, improved community engagement, student-driven initiatives and momentum towards improved Aboriginal student outcomes.

To some degree, addressing leadership issues is beyond the purview of the average teacher surviving the day-to-day pressures of teaching. However, reminding executive and staff that Aboriginal education is a state and national priority and that implementing successful initiatives can reap benefits for themselves and the school, can be one way to build momentum.

Developing and connecting with allies including executive members is prudent and practical. Small but strategic and impactful steps, such as posting students' work on an Aboriginal topic on the school's website or in the newsletter, can build momentum, capacity, and broader interest. This also shows the community your commitment to making a difference. Getting students and colleagues to 'buy in' is crucial in building a critical mass to influence change at the top. And let's not forget the real leaders of Aboriginal education in our schools, AEOs and Aboriginal staff. They are often quietly chipping away at barriers that we don't see or experience. Supporting and creating opportunities for these middle leaders is critical for any real change in schools and they can often leverage community support and engagement far better than most teachers can.

END OF CHAPTER REFLECTION

Identify three hurdles and three strategies for implementing Aboriginal education (whether it be curriculum, teaching strategies, policies, whole school reform etc.) in your classroom and/or school.

_____

_____

_____

_____

_____

_____

_____

_____

_____

_____

Use the following table to identify and unpack these hurdles

	What do you do well? What is holding you back?	What could you improve? What do you need to support improvement?	What opportunities are available? How can you leverage these?	What are the personal risks to overcoming these barriers?
Hurdle 1				
Hurdle 2				
Hurdle 3				

Now use the table to think about strategies to overcome the barriers.

	What resources will help? Where/how can you get these?	If you can't get the resources you need, what can you do instead?	How can you turn your strengths into strategies?	What are the systemic risks and how might you overcome these?
Strategy 1				
Strategy 2				
Strategy 3				

After reflecting on this analysis, think about the one 'overarching' strategy that will make the most difference and that you can implement soon. What is it and how would you go about implementing it?

_____

_____

_____

_____

_____

Who might be your allies in implementing this strategy and how will you work together to affect change?

_____

_____

_____

_____

_____

_____

Chapter Eight

FROM SURFACE TO DEEP LEVEL LEARNING

An important question we need to ask ourselves is how do we move from tokenistic, surface-level Aboriginal perspectives to embedding an Aboriginal curriculum narrative into our teaching and learning?

Unpacking Curriculum

When we think about curriculum, what comes to mind? Generally, we see curriculum as the content we are teaching in the classroom, content that is determined by a syllabus, a syllabus that is constructed by an accreditation institution that sits outside of schools. So, in many ways, what we teach is determined by 'others' outside the daily practice of teaching.

Significantly, curriculum represents what is considered valuable and essential knowledge - what information and skills do we think kids need to know and have to participate in society beyond school? Economic concerns through employment-ready approaches have increasingly dominated education policies and debates and so we are increasingly driven by market forces rather than by why many of us became teachers – to make a difference in kids' lives, particularly those marginalised by the system (Burgess et al., 2022a).

The knowledge presented through the curriculum is predominantly western, Eurocentric and monocultural, underpinned by Christian values and narratives. In this sense then, the knowledge represents the world 'outside' the classroom and an accumulation of this knowledge is perceived as necessary for future success (Burgess et al., 2022a). Therefore, the knowledge presented in schools is largely representational and transactional.

This of course raises questions about what and whose knowledge is selected, how it is taught, assessed and evaluated. The impact that this has on individual and collective knowledges, values and identities determines the shape of our society, including levels of social inclusion and cohesiveness. Ironically, in the last two to three decades, our international test results (PISA) have decreased as inequity has increased (Teach for Australia, 2019) and yet governments fail to acknowledge and seriously address equity, despite the best efforts of many schools and teachers.

An important point here is student assessment – what, how and why. If the knowledge presented is culturally biased, then the results will also be biased. It's little wonder then, that those kids who don't come from middle class, English-speaking, Christian families don't necessarily have access to the cultural and social capital necessary for educational success. Implementing Aboriginal perspectives in the curriculum is a good example here. While more and more teachers and schools are embracing Aboriginal content in their programs, this knowledge is often not assessed unless it is central to the unit of work.

The implicit message to students and their parents is that Aboriginal knowledge is not as valuable as the assessed knowledge, that the Aboriginal topic was interesting and fun but not important. Until we centre Aboriginal content in assessment, then the 'bolted on' rather than 'built in' approach will continue.

Let's get back to that question of what knowledge is, who constructs it and why. Western knowledge is presented as classified, scientific, objective, impersonal, evidence-based and reductive. Concepts are reduced to minor pieces, and then constructed and connected to form a whole. Conversely, Indigenous knowledges centre on Country, kin, culture and community and so understanding the relational connections between these is key. Here, the whole is the starting point, and understanding the minor pieces occurs through these relational connections rather than information about each of these knowledges as separate entities. In summary, western curriculum is representational and transactional and is about *knowing*; Indigenous curriculum is relational and interactional and is about *being* and *doing*. Those essential differences influence the what, who and why of curriculum structure and content (Burgess et al., 2022a).

Thus, the construction of curriculum as an assortment of separate disciplines or subject areas provides the biggest challenge for teachers attempting to embed Aboriginal content into their programs. For kids, the challenge continues to be making relational connections between the various subjects to see the relevance of what they are learning to their everyday lives. Moreover, as these subjects are generally structured in competition with each other as faculty areas lobby for student numbers, making meaningful and innovative connections across faculty areas can be challenging.

Understanding these key ideas and issues is useful when thinking about how to identify and include Aboriginal content in your curriculum. Considering how to teach (i.e. your pedagogical approach) as well as what to teach is key, because in some subject areas where Aboriginal content is not obvious, a relational pedagogical approach that focusses on connections, interactions and inclusivity will engage a diverse range of students including Aboriginal students. Yarning circles, for instance, facilitate creative thinking, problem solving and intercultural communication, as long as they are carefully thought out to ensure everyone has the opportunity to participate.

Options, Not Orders!

In Australia, states and territories develop their own curriculum within the parameters of the Australian curriculum or adopt the Australian curriculum as is (the latest version at the time of writing in 2022, is Version 9.0). This national curriculum also includes an Aboriginal and Torres Strait Islander Histories and Cultures Cross-Curriculum Priority (CCP) and two other CCPs for implementation across all key learning areas. Initially slated to be mandatory, they were later deemed 'options not orders' (Australian Curriculum and Assessment Reporting Authority, 2014). Consequently, teachers who lack confidence in this area and/or struggle with the content knowledge and means by which to teach this, will not include it in their programs (see Chapter 7).

The Aboriginal and Torres Strait Islander CCP consists of three key elements: Country/Place; Culture; People, with a focus on identity and 'living communities'. Placing identity at the centre reinforces the significant role of this in Aboriginal student learning. Identifying Aboriginal communities as 'living communities' is important because it moves away from narratives that position Aboriginal people in the past to positioning them as central to living, continuous and dynamic communities. While the original CCP had only one of nine organising ideas (OI.6) that mention 'experiences viewed through historical, social and political lenses' the latest version (9) has provided more depth to this.

For example:

> (OI.3) *Aboriginal and Torres Strait Islander Peoples have holistic belief systems and are spiritually and intellectually connected to the land, sea, sky and waterways.*

> is now

(A_TSICP3) *The First Peoples of Australia are the traditional owners of Country/Place, protected in Australian Law by the Native Title Act 1993 which recognises pre-existing sovereignty, continuing systems of law and customs, and connection to Country/Place. This recognised legal right provides for economic sustainability and a voice into the development and management of Country/Place.*

There is now a greater acknowledgement of the impact of colonisation, Aboriginal responses to this, and the importance of the struggle for and achievement of economic, social, cultural and political rights. This is an important step given the conservative backlash to the curriculum review (see SMH 2022) and provides opportunities for a broader and deeper approach to Aboriginal content. Even so, as teachers, we should be asking how and where to include the following:

- truth-telling, Aboriginal voice

- past and present relationships between Aboriginal and non-Aboriginal people

- analysis of misrepresentation and misinformation about Aboriginal peoples, cultures and histories

- institutional/systemic discrimination and casual/individual racism - issues that are consistently raised by Aboriginal students and parents, often the major factor in leaving or changing schools

- complex issues such as sovereignty, treaty, self-determination, resistance, resilience

- current issues such as the Uluru Statement of the Heart, Northern Territory intervention, deaths in custody, health and education inequities

- critical, creative and evaluative thinking, multi-perspective problem-solving.

These are critical issues given the current Labor government's (from May 2022) commitment to implementing the Uluru Statement of the Heart. How can our children, and indeed many adults, engage meaningfully in and contribute to the conversation if their education does not prepare them for this? This is why as teachers, our role is so critical to the survival of democracy and civil society.

What Knowledges, Understandings and Skills Do We Need?

The following information is general to help frame some key concepts in Aboriginal knowledges, understandings, and skills. However, as teachers we need to ask local Aboriginal community members and knowledge holders how we can localise these, what knowledges can and can't be used and how we might deliver these in culturally appropriate and engaging ways. They are by no means comprehensive but a place to start your learning journey.

Aboriginal Knowledges

These points help us and our students understand the breadth, depth and diversity of Aboriginal knowledges, to think about the concepts underpinning these and how we might introduce them to our students in culturally appropriate and engaging ways. They are by no means comprehensive but a place to start our learning journey.

1. The significance of Aboriginal people's relationship to land, to their Country. Country describes the relational connections Aboriginal people have with land, seas and skies, and includes the human and non-human. Country is considered by Aboriginal people as a holder of knowledge and the essence of Aboriginality. This includes a deep connection and obligation to Country and how this relationship directs Aboriginal ways of being, doing and knowing. Issues such as sovereignty, treaty, land rights and native title are all important discussions to have in relation to this.

2. The power of the Dreaming which includes signposts for living, guiding yarns for children such as safety warnings or moral lessons for life. These are key learnings for surviving an often-harsh environment and are passed down through generations. All cultures have critical intergenerational messages, protocols and expected behaviours. Interesting lessons will explore these without trivialising the methods or messages.

3. The importance of local Aboriginal history and opportunities to develop a shared history. Aboriginal

children consistently report that while they are interested in general Aboriginal history such as well-known people and events, what they really want to hear about is the local history, events, and peoples of their area. For instance, if the Freedom Rides went through their town, what happened, who was involved, what was the impact locally of this event? Aboriginal kids often know someone in their community who has lived through some of these major events and say they would much prefer to listen to these yarns than what they read in textbooks (Burgess & Cavanagh, 2013). Understanding these local events and the people involved, can also help us understand past and present relationships between Aboriginal and non-Aboriginal people.

4. What are the issues that are important in the local Aboriginal community that could be included in the curriculum? For example, in some communities it may be chronic health issues and so many community activities may centre around health promotion and education, whereas another community might have high unemployment, so the focus is on education, training and innovative pathways to employment. Often issues such as racism and discrimination arise and so this provides opportunities to discuss and understand how they operate and how to counteract these. Through this you can support the community by raising awareness with your students.

Aboriginal Understandings

These key points help us help students develop a deeper understanding about Aboriginal peoples, histories and cultures, and how these should be ethically and respectfully engaged with.

1. Local cultural customs are alive and practised by many families. Often these practices are 'invisible' outside the community and so many people do not realise that they exist. The common stereotype we often hear in staff rooms is that Aboriginal kids in our schools don't know their culture. It is astounding that Aboriginal kids are often expected to know everything about their culture, and yet other kids are not questioned about their culture. In fact, students of Anglo-Australian backgrounds are often the most culturally illiterate (as are some teachers) but this never raises any questions. The reclamation and revival of local languages is an important step in many communities to visibilising their culture.

2. Diversity is a key concept that students need to understand, particularly in relation to Aboriginal peoples, communities, and voices. In most communities, Aboriginal people not only come from that Country but also from other areas, thus living 'off Country'. Like any community, this then produces a wide range of ideas and opinions.

3. Often, when a well-known Aboriginal person expresses an opinion on national media, audiences often think that this represents all Aboriginal people, even

though this assumption does not necessarily extend to other groups. So, facilitating diverse experiences for your students is important to engage their critical thinking skills and develop deeper understandings of Aboriginal peoples, cultures and histories.

4. The importance of cultural knowledge for all students to learn and grow is a key understanding. Aboriginal and non-Aboriginal students need to have cultural knowledge and recognise and respect the cultural knowledge of others as the basis for understanding a whole host of issues that affect our lives. This is an important tool for understanding and unpacking misinformation and misrepresentations of different cultural groups and thinking about counternarratives to talk back to these. Again, this employs key problem-solving skills involving critical and creative thinking.

5. Historically (and still today), Aboriginal peoples' knowledge and expertise have been appropriated by non-Aboriginal researchers and teachers often for their own use without proper permissions, acknowledgement and even accurate interpretation. It is important that we, as teachers, model ethical and respectful behaviour by acknowledging individual and community ownership of cultures and histories and ask permission to use these. Without this, goodwill between communities and schools can be undermined.

Aboriginal Skills

The third area in understanding Country and enacting this in curriculum is understanding and knowing the skills that we need to work with Aboriginal people. These are a starting point in developing your cross-cultural communication skills.

1. Deep listening to Country and Aboriginal voices is a key skill - not just the listening we tend to do on the run as busy teachers, but reflective and contemplative consideration of what is being conveyed. It is described by author, Miriam-Rose Ungunmerr-Baumann (Healing Foundation, 2014), as:

    > *A special quality. A unique gift of the Aboriginal people is inner deep listening and quiet still awareness. Dadirri recognises the deep spring that is inside us. It is something like what you call contemplation. The contemplative way of Dadirri spreads over our whole life. It renews us and brings us peace. It makes us feel whole again* (p. 139).

    This often includes lengthy silences that can be uncomfortable and/or feel time-consuming. This challenges us to move beyond surface interaction to a deeper level of engagement with Aboriginal Country and people, to go the extra mile to better understand what the community is trying to tell us. Providing truth-telling opportunities to listen to Aboriginal lived experiences requires deep listening and helps move beyond surface level engagement.

2. Local protocols and cross-cultural communication skills include verbal and non-verbal gestures which are often learnt through experience. Your first step in this process is to have a yarn with Aboriginal staff such as AEOs, teachers, administration staff if they are at your school, or Aboriginal parents. If not available, then system support such as Aboriginal education consultants and/or Aboriginal community consultants and the local AECG are great to connect with.

   There are some protocols which are more broadly used such as using Aunty and Uncle as a sign of respect to an Elder (though you shouldn't assume as a non-Aboriginal person that you can use this so check with a trusted Aboriginal staff or community member). In some communities when a person has passed, it is customary not to use that person's name for a period but rather a generic term such as 'grandfather' in language. Again, as a local protocol you should seek advice as to what practice demonstrates respect.

3. Accurately acknowledging and accessing local knowledge and expertise needs to occur in a way that is acceptable to the community. Moreover, accepting the community's right to place caveats around certain knowledges or practices, such as the general understanding that women are not allowed to play the yidaki (didgeridoo) in most, if not all communities, is an important skill here.

   Mostly, Aboriginal people are happy to share knowledges with you particularly if it will help students understand Aboriginal cultures and histories. Better still, having

Aboriginal community members in your classroom, where you are a learner alongside your students, is a powerful way to acknowledge Aboriginal expertise and cultural wealth and challenge the power relationships that students often see between communities and schools.

4. Collaborative, inclusive interactions with Aboriginal families and communities that reflect a respectful approach is an important skill. This is achieved through building trust relationships with Aboriginal families and community members that demonstrate a commitment to working respectfully with each other. It can also mean openly admitting when you are wrong and working towards making amends to keep dialogue open and relationships positive.

   Reciprocity is important here. Giving back to the community will demonstrate your trust and respect in the relationship. Remember, Aboriginal people and other marginalised communities are often suspicious of institutions which have excluded them in the past and contributed to their oppression, so be prepared to be challenged and react with honesty and humility rather than offence or indignation.

END OF CHAPTER REFLECTION

Describe the aspects of your curriculum that you enjoy teaching the most.

_____

_____

_____

_____

How does an understanding of the way in which curriculum is structured in our western system, help us think about how we might *Indigenise* the curriculum?

_____

_____

_____

_____

_____

If you could make any changes to what and how you teach, what would they be?

_____

_____

_____

_____

How would you apply local Aboriginal knowledges, understandings and skills to your curriculum and pedagogy?

_____

_____

_____

_____

_____

Mind Map

Fill in the mind map below or create one of your own. Identify general and/or local Aboriginal knowledges, understandings and skills that could help you construct a Unit of Work.

You can add points from the Aboriginal and Torres Strait Islander CCP in each of the sections if they fit.

Think about an assessment task where students can demonstrate what knowledges, understandings, and skills they have learnt along the way.

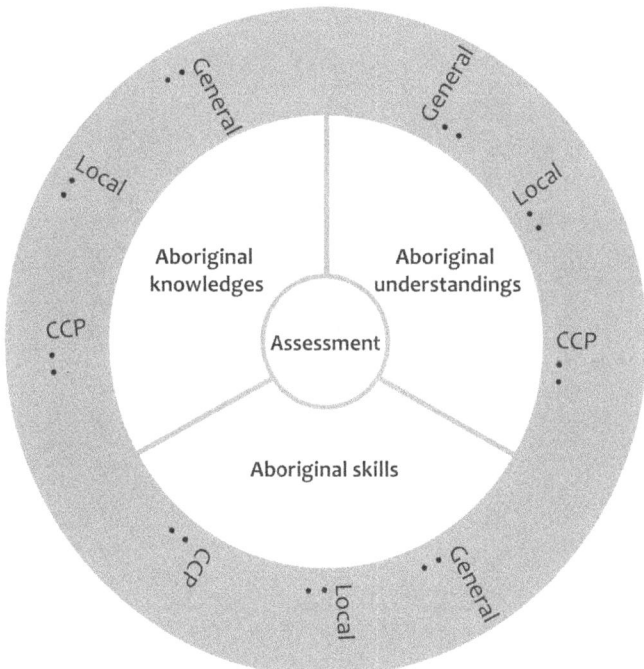

Chapter Nine

LEARNING FROM COUNTRY

What do we mean by the term Country? It is Aboriginal English (different from Standard Australian English) word that describes land as a living entity, the essence of Aboriginality and includes relational connections to people, culture, spirituality, history, environment, and ecologies of the non-human world. This can be understood through Aunty Laklak Burarrwanga (2013), a Datiwuy Elder, Caretaker for Gumatj:

> *Country has many layers of meaning. It incorporates people, animals, plants, water, and land. But Country is more than just people and things, it is also what connects them to each other and to multiple spiritual and symbolic realms. It relates to laws, custom, movement, song, knowledges,*

relationships, histories, presents, futures, and spirit beings. Country can be talked to, it can be known, it can itself communicate, feel, and take action. Country for us is alive with story, law, power, and kinship relations that join not only people to each other but link people, ancestors, place, animals, rocks, plants, stories and songs within land and sea. So you see knowledge about Country is important because it's about how and where you fit within the world and how you connect to others and to place (p. 54).

Galarrwuy Yunupingu, Chairman of the Northern Land Council (2007), draws attention to the importance of land to Aboriginal people, and the inappropriate western way of placing an economic value on everything:

For Aboriginal people there is literally no life without the land. The land is where our ancestors came from in the Dreamtime, and it is where we shall return. The land binds our fathers, ourselves and our children together. If we lose our land, we have literally lost our lives and spirits, and no amount of social welfare or compensation can ever make it up to us (p. 1).

Another way to think about this is to consider Professor W. E. H. Stanner, who famously wrote these words in 'White Man Got No Dreaming' (1979, p. 230):

No English words are good enough to give a sense of the links between an Aboriginal group and its homelands. Our word "home", warm and suggestive though it be, does not match the Aboriginal word that may mean "camp", "hearth", "country", "everlasting home", "token place", "life source", "spirit centre", and much else all in one. Our word "land" is too spare and meagre...the Aboriginal would speak of "earth" and use the word in a richly symbolic way to mean his shoulder or his side. I have seen an Aboriginal embrace the earth he walked on. To put our words "home" and "land" together into "homeland" is a little better but not much. A different tradition leaves us tongueless and earless towards this other world of meaning and significance.

This highlights the difficulty of translating complex Aboriginal concepts and signposts how and why misunderstandings, misinformation and misconceptions have emerged and undermined Aboriginal and non-Aboriginal relationships.

Songlines

Dr Aunty Lyn Riley et.al., (2022) draw on their knowledge and experiences of local Songlines as they explain:

Songlines are complex pathways that explain the history and meaning of spiritual, ecological, economic, environmental, cultural, and ontological knowledge that is written in the Land. Each verse records significant events, understandings and meanings at a particular site and is repeated several times. Aboriginal Elders and traditional owners travel along Songlines with their young people, telling the stories and singing the songs of the sites, so that children acquire a mental map of their Country, the boundaries of Clan and Nation groups and trade routes throughout the Country (p. 70).

The most important understanding you will hear about Country will be from your local Aboriginal community who will use their own protocols, Songlines and stories to explain the way in which they want you to understand it.

Place-Based Learning

Understanding Country and Songlines provides opportunities for place-based learning, where your students can understand the world by first making deep connections to local places. This not only works for Aboriginal students but many students. An Aboriginal teacher who completed Learning from Country with us at Sydney University talks about how she uses the concept of place to connect with her largely multicultural and refugee students. She says that they share their experiences of place, of leaving their homelands and coming to a new place. They want to know about the place they are now living on through Aboriginal understandings of place. This helps them build connections to Country, to each other, and to the school.

It reinforces that every place has a complex and contested history and that providing opportunities to understand and discuss these histories of place builds critical consciousness, supports healing and creates opportunities for new place-based yarns that belong to us all. This sharing of knowledge creates an inclusive classroom where every student has a story and a role to play, as well as the confidence to be critical and creative thinkers as we unpack the complexities of place. Engaging with local Aboriginal community members to learn on and from Country helps all of us learn, grow, and share.

Invite Truth-Telling to Foster Belonging

One of the hesitations for teachers is knowing that teaching Aboriginal histories and issues through truth-telling (see for instance https://www.reconciliation.org.au/reconciliation/truth-telling/) often includes difficult, uncomfortable, complex and controversial issues, so questions teachers may have could include:

1. Are my students ready for this?

2. Am I ready to teach this area and can I answer their questions? What do I do if I can't?

3. What terminology do I use? Will I inadvertently say something offensive? What can and can't I talk about?

4. Where will I get sufficient information with enough depth and breadth to make it meaningful and how will I know if it is authentic and accurate?

5. Who should I ask in the local community?

Engage, Embrace and Enact

1. It is surprising how much kids can absorb and understand from a young age. Presented in age-appropriate ways like any material, children in the early years are learning about wrong/right, good/bad and the immediate world they live in such as family, school, and community, and so connections can be made at this level.

If Aboriginal content is scoped, sequenced, and scaffolded as you do for any other subject, it is possible to build and develop a coherent narrative for you and the kids by storying local cultures, histories, and lived experiences that all kids can engage with and relate to.

If you have Aboriginal students in your class, you should talk with them discreetly to see if they are ready to listen to a potentially upsetting presentation as well as liaise with their families.

If there is an AEO in the school, this would be the first person to talk to, including what strategies you might employ to support any students dealing with distress, turmoil or anger.

Preparation and debriefing is a critical part of the overall process and important so that the intended lessons are learnt. See the Healing Foundation's Stolen Generations Resource Kit for Teachers and Students

2. Are we ever ready to teach anything?
    One of the simultaneously exciting and scary things about teaching is its unpredictability. We can plan, prepare, have a plan b, c and d and yet the unexpected can throw everything into chaos. But making a difference never comes without angst, doubts, and a bit of craziness.

    It's worth considering in this context how to deal with the difficult, uncomfortable, and complex issues in this learning area - these are important issues and emotions can be unpredictable and intense.

What we know is that by and large, Aboriginal people don't want non-Aboriginal people to feel guilty and they don't blame them for the past. Rather, they want you and your students to listen deeply to the impact of colonisation on their lives and understand the consequent intergenerational trauma. Embracing truth-telling and being part of the change is the key and as teachers we have a significant role to play in this.

An important lesson is that once you know you can't 'unknow', so to not do anything becomes a deliberate act of not caring and protecting the status quo.

3. Terminology comes up all the time as it can be an easy thing to get wrong and inadvertently offend Aboriginal people. The media often uses the wrong or offensive language but the ABC and SBS are usually accurate and include appropriate protocols in their programs and so they are a good source. Both also have education websites with resources. Correct terminology is available on several sites such as https://www.narragunnawali.org.au/about/terminology-guide.

4. There is a plethora of websites that offer information and resources on Aboriginal peoples, histories and cultures and so evaluating what is authentic and accurate and what is not, is critical. Rule of thumb is that government and reputable institutions such

as the Human Rights Commission are your best bet, and they often have links to direct you to other reputable sites.

If you are unsure, don't use. Incorrect and/or old terminology, talking about Aboriginal people as one group and other generalisations are good indicators that the information is problematic. They are usually pretty easy to spot once you know what you are looking for!

There are also key Aboriginal agencies such as AIATSIS which also provide information and access to the latest resources and research. If you want to have a good overview of the landscape, get a copy of 'The Little Red Yellow Black Book' from AIATSIS. (See also Chapter Eleven).

5. Identifying who to talk to in the community can be a key concern for teachers, particularly if there are few or no Aboriginal students in the school. However, starting with your student population and talking to their parents is an important protocol to observe. If you have an AEO or staff member, ask them first as they usually have a good overview and insight into the local Aboriginal community. They can steer you in the right direction and/or provide the introductory link between you and the community. If there is no-one to talk to at the school level, contact your relevant education system personnel as a starting point. You could also find out if other schools in the area are active in Aboriginal education and contact them.

Becoming part of a supportive network will make a big difference and could help you avoid common pitfalls. For instance, you could check if your local council has an Aboriginal advisory group, national parks generally have Aboriginal rangers and other government agencies such as health often have Aboriginal workers.

If you are in NSW there is likely to be a local AECG whose primary role is to work with schools, and a local Aboriginal land council which may also have educational and cultural programs as well as provide more contacts.

Regardless of your context, you will need to put the leg work in yourself to build relationships and trust if you want community involvement in your teaching.

Importantly;

One: don't rely on just one person to represent the community, you need to listen to a range of people and be mindful of, but not involved in, local politics.

Two: use local cultural protocols to address people, introduce yourself and act appropriately in community contexts.

Three: demonstrate genuine interest by building your knowledge of the history of colonisation and its impact on Aboriginal peoples and cultures, particularly in the local community.

It's an interesting phenomenon that Aboriginal stories of trauma and tragedy can nurture a sense of belonging as the listener simultaneously feels vulnerable and included in the story. The strong and generous message is that you can't change the past but as teachers you can make a difference for the future.

Teachers who have had Stolen Generation survivors in their classroom overwhelmingly speak about the impact on their students and the positive change in the way in which students talk about and engage with Aboriginal histories and cultures.

Localise Your Curriculum by Learning from Country

So we return to the question - *how do we move from tokenistic, surface-level Aboriginal perspectives to embedding an Aboriginal curriculum narrative into our teaching and learning?*

When thinking about and planning Aboriginal content, you need to engage at the local level. As every school is on Country, knowing what this is, and acknowledging this in various ways, signals that you respect Aboriginal peoples, cultures, and histories. Yarning with Aboriginal staff, students, families, and communities will help you learn about local cultures, histories and issues, and build relationships in the community.

Learning from Country means experiencing local cultures and histories by *walking with* and *listening to* local Aboriginal community members on Country. It is important to note that Country is everywhere - in urban centres as well as in rural locations. Stereotypes often relegate 'real Aborigines' to the 'outback, desert or bush' but Aboriginal cultures and peoples live in complex, dynamic and cultured communities in cities, suburbs, and regional areas. Many sites in these areas are spaces of resistance, resilience, and revitalisation, visible through street art, murals, community centres, Aboriginal organisations, sports clubs, museums, art galleries and performance spaces (Thorpe et al., 2021).

By listening to Aboriginal voices, doing some research, and engaging locally, you can educate yourself and develop a shared history with your students so everyone can participate and connect to Aboriginal content in the curriculum.

The relationship between Aboriginal and non-Aboriginal people over time is an important consideration because if you don't understand this, and the ways in which institutions such as governments, schools, and the media have influenced this, then it's difficult to understand where we are today, and why and how we can change this.

To help us understand what Aboriginal and non-Aboriginal people think about these issues, Reconciliation Australia produces a survey called the Australian Reconciliation Barometer. This *'measures attitudes towards reconciliation, using the five dimensions of reconciliation—race relations, equality and equity, unity, institutional integrity, and historical acceptance'*. It reminds us of how far we have come and how much further we must go. It lays bare our educational gaps and reinforces that many non-Aboriginal people haven't met an Aboriginal person and therefore are influenced by the media and other second-hand information.

This is where concepts such as truth-telling and shared history can be so important. Truth-telling respectfully acknowledges Aboriginal peoples' experiences and responses to colonisation. Making this history visible in the relationships you build and the pedagogical work you do, creates a sense of belonging for Aboriginal kids who see themselves reflected in the curriculum.

A shared history is about understanding and analysing the relationship between Aboriginal and non-Aboriginal people not through the lens of shame or guilt but through one of making a difference, so we can change the narrative one student at a time. Once the narrative changes, people start to engage and connect. For instance, when the federal Labor party was elected in 2022, they immediately positioned the 'Uluru Statement of the Heart' at the centre of the national conversation, and so attention to issues impacting on Aboriginal and Torres Strait Islander peoples was revived.

The Learning from Country (LFC) Framework (see Figure 1) is designed to understand and initiate the processes for developing an Aboriginal curriculum where teachers and students can learn together from Country and Aboriginal voices. It is an ethical position that centres Aboriginal people and Country as foundational to educational experiences. It demonstrates a commitment to building relationships, healing past wrongs, and moving forward in respectful partnerships to make change.

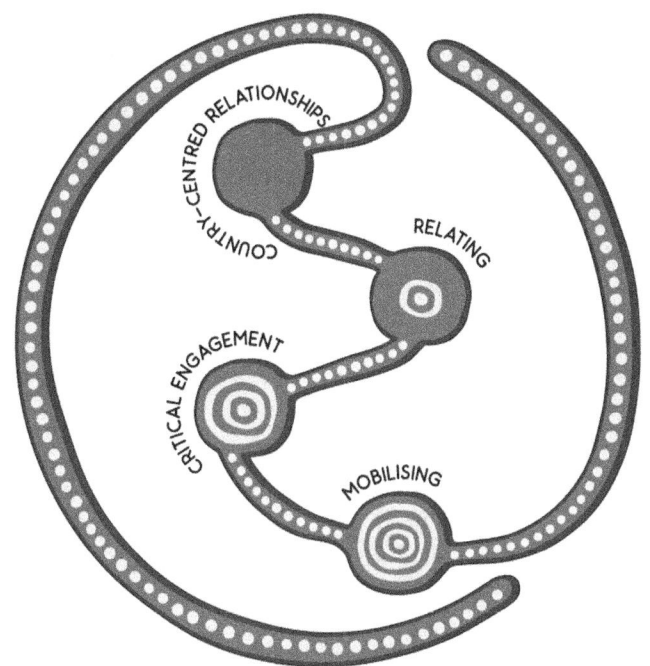

Figure 1
Learning from Country Framework

The framework (Burgess et al., 2022b) can be described as a metaphor that:

> *is designed around bodies of water, a significant feature of the Country where this framework originated. The first waterhole is dark blue and respects that Country is strong and 'full' of knowledge. The light blue circles represent new and cumulative knowledge acquired through deep listening to Aboriginal community voices and truth-telling. As new knowledge is absorbed, reflected upon and shared, it flows through each waterhole, growing into an Aboriginal*

curriculum narrative. This process is non-linear, reflexive and nurtures belonging.

The framework identifies four processes that are relational, reflective and cyclical. This includes:

1. ***Country-centred relationships*** *– Respect through deep listening to Aboriginal voice*

2. ***Relating*** *– Connect to Country through truth-telling and nurture belonging*

3. ***Critical Engagement*** *– Reflect on Country-centred relationships to develop critical consciousness and share knowledge*

4. ***Mobilising*** *– Direct through employing culturally sustaining and nourishing practices*

How Do We Use This Framework?

The framework provides a process in which to build a relational and holistic curriculum that challenges the categorised nature of discipline-based western knowledge. In western systems, the starting point is knowledge production based on scientific and rational thought.

The LFC Framework, however, starts with Aboriginal protocols and values, such as how to respectfully introduce ourselves to parents and communities. They will want to get to know you as a person as an early but critical step in relationship building.

Showing respect by deep listening and patience to understand where families are coming from, is vital for the next step.

Connecting to Country through Aboriginal community is the second process in developing your relationships. Providing space for truth-telling such as organising yarning sessions with staff and/or inviting community to share experiences with students can create relational connections that include everyone. A sense of belonging is needed to move onto the next step of developing a critical consciousness for deeper understanding, reflection and respect.

The third process harnesses truth-telling to encourage critical engagement with these new knowledges. Uncomfortable, emotional, and new experiences prompt a journey of reflection to develop a shared body of knowledge that will contribute to our curriculum narrative. This process will build on our Country-centred relationships and open up new paths to learning.

Finally, as we come to understand the relational connections between Country, community, Aboriginal knowledges, and our curriculum and pedagogical practices, we can enact holistic and inclusive classrooms. This then mobilises culturally nourishing learning experiences that engage, embrace and include all students.

The Learning from Country Framework aims to bring people together, prompting us to see ourselves in the bigger picture of an unsettled land still in tension with our past and in desperate need of healing. If we listen to, respect, and acknowledge the voices of the land and its first inhabitants, this healing is an opportunity to come together for a better and shared lifestyle.

Learning from Country is a ripple of optimistic grassroots change, an intergenerational project of belonging, nurturing and sustainability for nation building.

END OF CHAPTER REFLECTION

How might you use each of the processes in the Learning from Country Framework in your relationship building, curriculum narrative and/or culturally nourishing pedagogies?

Country-Centred Relationships

Relationship building

_____

_____

_____

Curriculum narrative

_____

_____

_____

_____

Culturally nourishing pedagogies

_____

_____

_____

_____

_____

Relating

Relationship building

_____

_____

_____

_____

_____

_____

_____

Curriculum narrative

_____

_____

_____

_____

_____

_____

_____

Culturally nourishing pedagogies

_____

_____

_____

_____

_____

_____

_____

Critical Engagement

Relationship building

_____

_____

_____

_____

Curriculum narrative

_____

_____

_____

_____

_____

_____

Culturally nourishing pedagogies

_____

_____

_____

_____

_____

Mobilising

Relationship building

_____

_____

_____

_____

_____

_____

_____

Curriculum narrative

Culturally nourishing pedagogies

Chapter Ten

PEDAGOGY THAT MAKES A DIFFERENCE

A fancy word for everyday teaching practice, pedagogy is one of those educational terms that you either relate to or don't, or like us, come to gradually after thinking about our teaching practices over time. While there are differing descriptions of pedagogy, it is generally thought of as a combination of teaching, learning and curriculum content.

Anglo-American traditions view pedagogy as a method focussing on the technical aspects of teaching, whereas European understandings include interactions and relationships between teachers and students. Early Childhood Australia (2014) suggests that pedagogy is *'about the connections between relationships, curriculum decision making and teaching and learning strategies. The word 'pedagogy' reminds educators of the centrality of relationships for learning.'*

This resonates with our understanding of pedagogy which also includes elements such as high expectations, holistic and relational approaches, and cultural responsiveness through the inclusion of children's cultural backgrounds. Teaching and learning doesn't occur in a vacuum but is influenced by these and other contextual factors. Therefore, pedagogy is more than just teaching and learning, and as teachers, we need to be mindful of context, including our own cultural positioning, potential biases, and ways of operating.

Aboriginal Ways of Knowing, Being and Doing

We often hear about concepts such as Aboriginal worldviews and ways of knowing, being and doing (Martin, 2005), but what do they mean? Karen Martin (2005), a Noonuccal, Quandamooka scholar explains what they mean to her:

> *To know who you are in relatedness is the ultimate premise of Aboriginal worldview because this is the formation of identity. This is acquired through being immersed in situations, contexts of people and other elements which lead us to come to see and to come to know, and then be part of the relatedness through change and past, present, and future (p. 28).*

When thinking about Aboriginal ways of knowing, being and doing, it can help to think of these in relation to western systems to get a sense of how and why certain groups are excluded and/or struggle to succeed. This can help us think about how we might incorporate Aboriginal ways in our teaching as well as provide Aboriginal students with tools to better understand western systems.

Aboriginal ways of knowing, being and doing are holistic, relational, and relationships-focussed (Burgess et al., 2022a). Generally speaking, this means seeing connections between various knowledges and actions as well as how to consider the whole before analysing the parts. This is done within a group-oriented, shared approach where everyone has a seat at the table rather than an identified leader making final decisions. Aboriginal groups aim for consensus on important issues which are more likely decided using cultural protocols, accountabilities, and obligations than by external direction or criteria. Expertise therefore, is not necessarily based on role, title, or education level, but on individual readiness through levels of experience and respect in the community. Finally, cyclical, and reflective approaches that respond to individual and group needs are prioritised over external criteria and deadlines.

Western ways of knowing, being and doing are quite different, and by understanding these, the impact of colonisation through government policies and actions can be more clearly understood. Where Aboriginal knowledge is relationships-focussed, western knowledge is information-focussed and is acquired and exchanged for something else such as an economic future beyond school. Individual rather than group success is rewarded. Western knowledge is hierarchical and understood by first learning the parts that make up the whole. Thus, knowledge is compartmentalised and delivered in predetermined levels such as age rather than on individual readiness (Burgess et al., 2022a). Decision-making is led by the boss who, while listening to others, is accountable for the final decision. The process is linear with little room or time for reflection and reconsideration after the decision is made.

Thus, if we think of this in terms of school contexts, we can see how Aboriginal students may find western ways of knowing, being and doing confusing and alienating and therefore struggle to engage and succeed. Rather than thinking that Aboriginal students and their cultures need to change to fit into the system, we as teachers should look for ways to manipulate the system to better meet the needs of Aboriginal kids and their families, while providing them with access to opportunities and success.

Relationships Before Rigour

Engaging classrooms are key - if you teach mostly from textbooks, talk *at* the students, introduce abstract concepts without offering some relevance, and don't utilise interactive, challenging and creative ways for students to 'discover' the answers themselves, then you will have classroom management issues.

Implementing Aboriginal curriculum and pedagogy can improve your teaching skills by:

- thinking 'outside the box' - what teaching/learning strategies will engage these kids?

- understanding that Aboriginal curriculum is place, time and issue responsive (textbook teaching therefore is limiting and limited),

- building trust relationships through understanding individual lived experiences outside of school,

- engaging with parents and community,

- demonstrating a personal interest in local community culture, identity, and current issues,

- including student's socio-cultural background in everyday practice,

- including local histories, cultures and Country/community in the curriculum,

- providing students with opportunities to express themselves in a variety of ways such as art, music, model building etc, and

- utilising yarning circles to encourage participation where the teacher is *part of* the circle, *not directing* it.

These tools combine to create culturally inclusive and safe classrooms, as they address the perceived invisibility of culture in educational settings. It helps us to think about the role of culture, and better understand our own culture and how it influences what we say and do. This is important because we may unintentionally exclude, offend, confuse or make students or colleagues feel uncomfortable.

Understanding cultural protocols such as modes of address, actions and behaviours, and the challenges and stresses for marginalised students trying to fit in, helps us establish appropriate and clear expectations and routines that are inclusive and positive.

Students who perceive themselves as 'outsiders' are likely to be wary, even defensive, having learnt to expect negative responses from others. So, when their reaction to something said or done appears excessive in the context - think about how weary they must be having these inbuilt defence systems constantly on alert.

Listen, be kind and attentive and support them on their journey through this. Reinforcing that every student has something important to contribute will automatically create a positive, trusting environment.

Successfully managing controversial issues should emerge in your teaching if you are encouraging critical thinking, problem solving and constructive dialogue. If you have created a safe and positive classroom, then this should be enough.

However, it is also good to have a few extra tools up your sleeve, such as:

- help students understand that 'knowledge truths' depend on culture, perception and experience. For instance, think of the contrast between Aboriginal and non-Aboriginal understandings of land,

- use experiential teaching, conceptual frameworks and teachable moments even if it means temporarily going off on a tangent,

- manage emotions to moderate discussion, insist on respecting opinions even if you don't agree,

- teach students how to address issues on an intellectual level,

- don't allow personal or cultural name-calling or stereotyping, and

- have a 'safety switch' you can employ that will distract and calm down any heated debate with an activity they all enjoy.

In saying this, be prepared to call out racism and other offensive behaviour because if you don't, students will lose trust and think you condone the behaviour. You will have to do this in a way that doesn't further inflame the situation – which is why knowing your students is critical.

Employing a Pedagogical Framework

A pedagogical framework or structure for teaching/learning is like a coat hanger to hang your curriculum content on, one that is flexible and can be reshaped as needed. There are many and varied frameworks available, but at the end of the day, these are ways of organising learning and mapping to check you have included the various curriculum requirements.

While the LFC Framework was explained in detail in Chapter Nine, other frameworks such as Bloom's Taxonomy, the NSW

Quality Teaching Framework (2003) and Yunkaporta's (2009) 8 Aboriginal Ways of Learning (Aboriginal Pedagogy) (see End of Chapter Reflection for links) are better known and also useful, accessible and support teachers in delivering their curriculum. They are either embedded in the way in which a syllabus is developed and/or available through teacher professional learning. What they have in common is how they resonate with your understandings and experiences of curriculum delivery and provide opportunities for developing Aboriginal content to your curriculum narrative.

END OF CHAPTER REFLECTION

List teaching strategies that you feel best engage all students.

_____

_____

_____

_____

List teaching strategies that specifically engage Aboriginal students or students who are often not interested in classwork.

_____

_____

_____

_____

_____

Look at one of the three frameworks mentioned:

Blooms Taxonomy (https://cft.vanderbilt.edu/guides-sub-pages/blooms-taxonomy/)

NSW Quality Teaching Framework (https://theelements.schools.nsw.gov.au/introduction-to-the-elements/policy-reforms-and-focus-areas/quality-teaching-framework.html)

8 Aboriginal Ways of Learning (https://www.8ways.online/)

Use this to develop engaging teaching/learning activities in a topic area that doesn't have Aboriginal content in it.

Topic: .... Assessment: ....

Framework(s) Applied	Teaching/Learning Strategies

Chapter Eleven

RESOURCES AND WHERE TO START

Fear of getting it wrong or offending often holds people back. Many don't know where to start and what to use when it comes to resources. It's scary we know, and is often the thing that stops many educators from moving forward and embedding culturally rich and authentic content in their programs. It's easy to stay at a surface level and not go deep into localising the curriculum out of fear of not knowing how to connect with the community and getting it wrong. What we suggest is to have a go and collaborate - you don't have to walk the journey alone.

We could name and endorse many organisations and websites; however, we know that things are forever changing so below is a summary of what to look for and things to avoid when it comes to selecting and using resources.

There are so many incredible resources available on the internet, however, it's important to never underestimate the value that local families and communities can offer. Remember that relationships don't happen overnight, and you as the educator will need to build those relationships before families and communities develop enough trust to add value to your teaching.

Where possible, always refer to resources in the local community that students can relate to. Think about all the things they can see, feel, and touch in their everyday lives.

Fictions and Stereotypes

Historically, Indigenous peoples here and overseas were relegated to the bottom of the human development ladder, a ladder that positioned northern European Caucasian men at the top (Bodkin-Andrews et al., 2014). After all, they created this ladder, which is why this still seeps into mainstream discourse.

However, these racial theories created fictions and stereotypes such as the 'noble or treacherous savage', a label used to justify the trafficking of skeletal remains to museums and universities of Europe, and dispossession from homelands (Bodkin-Andrews et al., 2014). In Australia, this dispossession was illegal and contravened orders from the motherland which stated that a treaty should be negotiated with the inhabitants of a newly 'discovered' territory. Thus, the 'savage' stereotype was particularly useful for justifying the unlawful dispossession of Aboriginal and Torres Strait Islander peoples from their lands. Demonising the 'natives' meant that settlers and farmers could justifiably defend land they had claimed with impunity (Dudgeon et al., 2014).

As frontier wars rolled out across the country, Aboriginal people were deemed a 'dying race' and a policy of protection was introduced to 'protect' the remaining population until they 'disappeared'. This also included diluting the Aboriginal 'race' by 'breeding out' the culture and colour and removing the children from Aboriginal families and placing them with white families, and/or in children's homes (Parbury, 2005). This cultural genocide continued until the late 1970s and many believe this continues today through the increasing number of Aboriginal children removed from their families and placed in 'Out of Home' care.

Stereotypes that accompanied these policies and actions still trickle through today, often trotted out by the media to sell a story. Children repeat these in the playground, employees in the workplace, and so casual racism still exists in many public spaces (Dudgeon et al., 2014).

Using Appropriate Resources

How do we know if a resource is accurate, appropriate, and effective? The first step is to identify the author, publisher, and year of publication. While it could be expected that an Indigenous author will present balanced views it cannot be assumed. Look for recommendations, testimonials, and authentication from respected people or agencies such as in NSW AECG, or the National Indigenous Artists Advocacy Association (NIAAA). The publication year is usually a clue to the context of the discourse and language and whether it is likely to be accepted in the current climate.

Terminology is often a clear indicator of the veracity of a resource. For example, if outdated terms such as 'Aborigines' or 'aboriginal people' (small caps), or more obvious ones like 'natives' or 'half-castes' are used then this is a good indicator that the information is inappropriate or biased.

Context is also important, so for example the term 'Blacks' is generally frowned upon here but common overseas, although more recently, 'Blak' is being used here, particularly by Aboriginal people. Terms such as 'blackfullas' can be appropriate if used by Aboriginal people but you need to consult with Aboriginal staff, students or parents to see what terms are acceptable in the local context.

Images can also be used inappropriately and send the wrong message. Make sure balanced images of Aboriginal peoples and cultures are in context, have appropriate captions and are accurately sourced. Include diverse and nuanced images as well as those that express leadership, self-determination, and independence. Political cartoons have a history of being both appropriate and inappropriate and so can provide rich material for exploration and discussion.

Oversimplifying, romanticising and trivialising Aboriginal peoples, cultures and histories contributes to inferior and disempowering treatment. These representations have at various times underpinned government policy, and negative comparisons with the non-Aboriginal population are still evident in some policies.

Examples of inaccuracies that continue to undermine Aboriginal content but still pop up in textbooks, curriculum, teaching programs and the media.

- Aboriginal people did not manage resources including food and water and so are not connected to any particular area of land and/or have no rights to it,
- Australian history started in 1788, through the process of discovery,
- Aboriginal people did not fight for their land, they died out due to disease,
- Aboriginal people have benefitted from western progress,
- Authentic Aboriginal culture only exists in the outback,
- Aboriginal people get 'special treatment' such as free housing, cars, as well as preference for jobs, university places etc,
- Aboriginal culture inhibits Aboriginal children's success at school,
- Aboriginal people have benefited from western education which guarantees them economic security,
- Aboriginal people are unreliable and/or are always late.

These are just some examples of the stereotypes we still hear in schools, from teachers and in general conversation. It is our responsibility as educators to call these out and, if possible, create teachable moments from these. The ABC program, 'You Can't Ask That' is a provocative program that might be worth sharing with colleagues to bring attention to some of the inappropriate comments about Aboriginal people, as well as other marginalised groups. It is a humorous and less confronting way of thinking about what we say and how we say it. It creates opportunities for important conversations.

Empowering Students

As teachers, we are the front line of challenging stereotypes and racism, and we can do so through the resources we select to teach with and, more importantly, the way in which we use and apply these. Significantly, a poor resource can be impactful in the classroom if it is used effectively.

For example, analysing old school textbooks to discuss how Aboriginal peoples and cultures are represented at this time is eye-opening for many kids. This helps them understand stereotypes or racist comments they might hear in the playground, at home or in the media by seeing where they came from. This then prompts conversations about what alternative, more accurate representations might look like, and how to construct arguments to include these.

A tactic we use in our mandatory Aboriginal education units at university is called 'Can o' Worms'. Here, we give students a strip of paper where they write down any question or comment they want to raise anonymously. They fold these up and put them in an envelope (can) and we pull out random comments at various times throughout the semester to stimulate discussion. This helps us assess student understanding of key issues as well as how to build their capacity to challenge myths and misunderstandings.

This is empowering for Aboriginal and non-Aboriginal students alike, and can build inclusiveness, camaraderie, and relevance of their learning to their everyday lives. Teaching strategies such as concept mapping, brainstorming, think-pair-share, jigsaw reading, debating, consequence webs etc. are all tools that help students deconstruct, reconstruct and build their own narrative about these complex areas.

Making Change - Making a Difference

Teaching critical thinking skills is important in all subjects as this challenges students to assess the accuracy and validity of sources. It includes thinking about where the source comes from, who wrote it, who benefits and who loses from its publication.

A good example of this is the media, which has become more brazen in promoting the populist views rather than a more balanced view of the issues. The concepts of 'fake news' and 'post truth' make for interesting ways to think about the common myths in Australian history, as well as current issues as they emerge. Every student, at some stage in their education, should have the opportunity to explore and critically analyse these if we hope to produce independent, critical thinkers who can engage with our democratic processes.

Analysing and critiquing relationships between texts, language, discourses, and social groups provides many opportunities for deconstructing and reconstructing resources and the information they provide. This is important to better understand the following:

- non-Aboriginal understandings of Aboriginal peoples, cultures, and histories and where these come from.
- Aboriginal students' understanding of themselves and their location in society.
- the development of relationships between Aboriginal and non-Aboriginal peoples.
- the origin, development and challenging of negative perceptions and deficit discourses.

Simultaneously, you as an educator can address many of these inaccuracies by teaching about:

- the true history of Australia beyond 1788.
- our shared history and the development of relationships between Aboriginal and non-Aboriginal people.
- the diversity of Aboriginal and Torres Strait Islander socio-cultural life.
- the true nature and ongoing impacts of colonisation.
- Aboriginal responses to colonisation such as protests, activism, advocacy, self-determination etc.
- stereotypes, ethnocentrism, inappropriate language and how to challenge these.
- Aboriginal achievements in diverse areas, including those important to Aboriginal communities but not necessarily visible to non-Aboriginal people.
- survival, resilience, self-determination, and autonomy.

Visual and performing arts, messaging through music, literature and picture books, film and television (fiction and nonfiction), and diverse media outlets are important and engaging sources of information for students to explore in the classroom. As many of these are developed by Aboriginal people, they provide more authentic, interesting, nuanced, and diverse representations of cultures and communities.

We as teachers can make a difference by selecting interesting, diverse, and challenging resources for students. The learning will be more impactful if they are given opportunities and encouraged to deconstruct, analyse and reconstruct their understandings and interpretations through a variety of mixed media. This is not limited to history or English classes but can be creatively applied across the full range of key learning areas, sending a strong message to students about the value of learning in this area.

Resources are complex and layered but as educators we have the opportunity and an obligation to expose our students to new ideas and concepts that challenge the 'norm' and help them better understand the complex world they live in.

AIATSIS has recently released (2022) a guide to evaluating and selecting education resources to help you do this work.

END OF CHAPTER REFLECTION

The University of Sydney Aboriginal Studies Library Guide is freely accessible to the general public and has links to a huge range of interesting and informative websites: **https://libguides.library.usyd.edu.au/aboriginalstudies.**

Think of a specific topic you plan to teach next term and use this site to see if you can locate Aboriginal content for this topic.

Topic ....

Useful website
URL: ....

Aboriginal Content

_____

_____

_____

_____

_____

Useful website
URL: ....

Aboriginal Content

_____

_____

_____

_____

_____

Locate an inappropriate image of Aboriginal people (these are not hard to find in a simple internet search).

URL and description of image:

_____

_____

_____

_____

Topic or lesson it could be applied to:

_____

Analysis of image:

_____

_____

_____

_____

_____

Teaching/learning activities to make this an important learning opportunity for students:

_____

_____

_____

_____

_____

Chapter Twelve

LEAD ABORIGINAL EDUCATION AND MAKE A DIFFERENCE

Consider this a call to action, a plea or even us begging you to open up your heart and mind to do more and understand that Australia needs your help to move towards a country that truly values Aboriginal Histories and Cultures; one that can heal from the ravages of colonisation.

Being that teacher who makes a difference requires more than just knowing your content and teaching it well. It's the work you do with students and communities that sets you apart from the rest. Schools and individual teachers who do a great job putting the community connections and wellbeing of the students first, often achieve the educational outcomes they desire. Sharing the responsibility and having a school-wide approach to improving educational outcomes filters down into every classroom and to every child. As educators, we must remember that every student and every family comes through the school gates with a story and an invisible backpack full of life experiences, cultures and sometimes trauma.

Leading Aboriginal education in schools is often left to one individual teacher and often the only Aboriginal staff member in the school. Other times it's a non-Aboriginal staff member who is the go-to for communities. This person understands the importance of consultation and having families on board as part of the decision-making process and teaching and learning of their child.

Throughout our collective educational experience, schools that focus their teaching and learning on a relationships-based framework get the best out of students. Principals and teachers sometimes come and go from the school community; however, the family groups and community often remain the same. The reputation of the school and the work they do is what keeps families and communities coming back, therefore it's important that there is more than one staff member doing the important work of engaging with communities.

Leading Practices That Make a Difference

Leadership is not necessarily about the title or position but consists of interconnected and thoughtful practices that can exist at all levels of the organisation. While the person at the top has authority and often the final say in key decisions, they may not necessarily be a leader. A leader is someone who you are prepared to follow, who leads by doing rather than by talking or promising and who makes you feel that your input is as important as their own. Leadership is based on reciprocal trust, relationships and experience, and in schools with substantive Aboriginal populations, often rests with the Aboriginal education workers or staff. They are often the people in the school most invested in the children and the community and therefore the school tends to look to them for guidance and advice.

The Critical Role of the Principal

Leadership practices occur in many ways and across many activities in a school and those that are relationships-focussed are more sustainable and responsive. These practices are not just individual but group practices that support overall school improvement. Even so, in this western system, the principal is critical, and we have all seen examples of the impact of good and bad principals.

Improved relationships lead to improved outcomes. We know this is the case when teaching students and this is also crucial for leaders to get the most out of their staff. The principal is responsible for leading the school and to engage and gain trust from staff, they must first focus on relationships. The style of leadership makes a difference and it's important that the principal continues to reflect on their leading practices to identify areas of improvement.

Working With Aboriginal Families and Communities

Engaging with, and connecting to parents and communities is an important, often underrated skill and leaders understand this. Engaging with marginalised families such as Aboriginal families is particularly tricky due to the weight of historical factors such as exclusion, alienation and trauma experienced at the hands of authorities. As teachers, we represent that authority whether we want to or not, and so we need to understand this in our interactions with families. Even so, it is important not to assume that this is the situation for all Aboriginal families and therefore you need to know your students and families so you can respond appropriately. Learning the familial connections in communities can also be helpful for identifying strategies and support for students. For instance, an Aunty or Nan might be a significant influence in a child's life and can thereby be an important person to talk to.

It's important to use cultural protocols and strength-based (rather than negative) language to demonstrate respect, understanding and genuine intentions. Visible signs of Aboriginality around the school and in the classroom such as flags, murals, posters, signage, children's work etc, also shows interest in Aboriginal cultures. This will support relationship building so you can share with your families, information about school structures, organisation and curriculum that empower parents to become involved in conversations, decision-making and school planning. Success comes from a willingness to adjust values, actions and outcomes and work as a team where leading practices are shared.

Developing Strategies and Practices

Working with Aboriginal students and their families to focus on what works as well as the end point helps develop a vision and plan for the future. Be the facilitator but not the expert as this demonstrates your belief in the child and their family as equal partners. Personal Learning Pathways are useful tools for doing this work as they accompany students from class to class, year to year and school to school. This provides opportunities for the student to reflect on and see the development of their future vision.

Communication is also the key, especially since we are in the business in Aboriginal education of challenging and changing a status quo that presents many hurdles for our students in reaching their potential. There will be resistance, racism and reactionary responses which require courageous conversations. As this year's NAIDOC theme says, Get Up, Stand Up, Show Up.

While we need to work with data, apply it in terms of value-added improvement rather than the number result. Remember, behind every statistic is a child with hopes and dreams like the rest of us, so keep this in mind when working with data. Don't let the pressure of gathering data and evidence undermine your knowledge and understanding of every child you teach, and your professional judgement on how best to help them be who they want to be.

Building communities of practice in your school can help grow and replenish the school's Aboriginal education strategy. Wenger (2000) suggests that a community of practice is a social learning system that creates a sense of belonging by developing a shared purpose, alignment between practices and imagination to create new possibilities. This joint enterprise of learning and leading creates productive interaction and a shared repertoire of concepts, language and tools in order to achieve common goals. Focussing on small steps, what is doable, and ongoing reflection of the processes and outcomes, will build the community of practice into a confident, competent and passionate team of advocates.

Indicators of success will emerge through actions rather than words such as engaged and motivated staff, increased family involvement and willingness to participate in and lead various school initiatives. There will be a sense of shared language, values and understandings based on educational, cultural, and social principles rather than hierarchies and rule following. The level of staff 'buy-in' is also an indicator of success and the higher the level, the more likely a community of practice emerges where belonging, optimism and relationships thrive.

Leadership and Leading

Consider the following scenario:

You arrive at your school which has a small Aboriginal student population and an 'ad hoc' approach to Aboriginal education. What do you do and where do you start? You are responsible for engaging Aboriginal students, families and the community in the school and know that this will make a big difference not only for this group of kids, but for the whole school.

There are five concurrent actions you can take to get started:

1. Get to know the community via the students and their families and engage in respectful conversations that value their opinions and ideas. Remember, local Aboriginal communities have been there as long if not longer than the school, they have seen good and bad teachers come and go, and have a wealth of untapped knowledge that could save you a lot of time and angst.

2. Seek out the staff members who are already doing good things and bring these people together in a meeting (or attend a prearranged meeting) and let them know they have your support. Listen to what they are already doing and any successes they may have had before suggesting or making changes. Encourage them to share their achievements and frustrations in a culturally safe space.

   Ask them what their vision for Aboriginal education is and put together a wish list with strategies to achieve these. Remind them that while these won't all be possible at least in the short-term, they are worth striving for. Suggest they create a vision board to keep motivated and on track and place this in a strategic location.

   Where possible, allocate time to achieve these goals, for instance an hour relief from class once a week or fortnight for the teacher who is driving the committee and these initiatives. Attend their meetings where possible and don't rely on just one person to do the reporting - find out how everyone is contributing.

3. Assess the data on Aboriginal students in terms of where they are currently at and where they need to be. Once you have this picture, consider what needs to be prioritised, what already exists and is working or not, and what initiatives you can consider.

   Don't just focus on the bottom. There are Aboriginal students who are doing well but perhaps could do better with targeted support such as extension programs, leadership opportunities etc. This group of students is often overlooked. High expectations for all students make a difference.

4. Position Aboriginal education in your whole school plan in ways that will facilitate the initiatives and strategies you wish to implement. This means explicitly naming these rather than using general statements. While there are obvious compliance and accountability elements to your plan, Aboriginal education continues to be a state and federal priority, so you are justified in taking the measures to meet these targets.

5. Implement targeted and impactful professional learning for all staff including office staff. To make real change you need whole school buy-in and commitment, which won't come at once but should be a key aim.

   Carefully assess what professional learning will be most effective. For instance, online cultural competency courses may have some value but are not as effective as Aboriginal-led and/or 'face-to-face' courses that are responsive to the audience. Like relationships-based teaching, relationships-based professional learning is most effective, especially when it is led by Aboriginal educators and community members.

Yarn with your local Aboriginal families and community members to see if they are interested in talking to teachers about local cultures and histories to build cultural awareness and culturally responsive teaching. The Learning from Country framework (Chapter Nine) might be useful here as an Aboriginal-inspired framework that will help scaffold professional learning processes and strategies.

Leadership and leading in schools in these current times is exhausting and you need to seek support where you can. If you don't already have a network of like-minded leaders, find one, join one. You will find them in other schools (obviously) but also in professional teachers' associations, for instance. Build strong advocacy in these networks and share the ups and downs. Remember, it takes a village, and your school is one of many in this village, and you can be a leader by making substantial, courageous and ethical decisions.

Shared Leadership

It's important to recognise that everyone in the school community has a role to play in the school improvement journey. A common misconception is that leadership and facilitating change is up to the principal and school executive. Whilst this is true, all the pieces of the puzzle need to fit before real change starts to take place. Sustainable change usually grows from the bottom up.

In many schools, the AEO is a significant leader in balancing relationships between students, families, communities, teachers, and principals. Without their unerring support, principals would be overwhelmed with the complexities of Aboriginal education. Support staff and administration staff are also important. It's critical that their views and opinions are included and valued, and that they are appreciated for the support they give. If they are not aware of their role in Aboriginal education, ensure they have access to professional learning.

Leading is a tricky business of balancing clear, confident decision-making with attentive listening and acknowledging the expertise and opinions of others that may differ from yours. Humility, vulnerability, and deference are strengths, not weaknesses, and leveraged strategically will be powerful allies in bringing about inclusive and effective change.

END OF CHAPTER REFLECTION

What are three things you can implement now to support Aboriginal education at your school?

_____

_____

_____

_____

Who can you reach out to for support?

_____

_____

_____

_____

What key departmental or systemic documents are most important when strategising in Aboriginal education?

_____

_____

_____

_____

_____

What key documents from other government and/or Aboriginal agencies might be of use in thinking more broadly and creatively about leading change?

_____

_____

_____

_____

_____

What change do you hope to see in the next 12 months?

Design your vision board here, indicating where your team can enhance and add their ideas and visions.

SUMMARY

We hope you enjoyed the information shared in this book and that you'll find it useful in your teaching practice.

You are educators and do an incredible job in showing up each and every day to make a difference. There will be many lives you change and shape throughout your career.

Thank you for choosing teaching as your profession. We hope you know just how special and valued you are.

There are many deadly educators and resources out there sharing knowledge and inspiring many. Learn and share your practice with others, never walk this journey alone.

An important message we really want you to take away from this book is the importance of self-care. You are loved and valued and must always remember that to show up and be that teacher, you must put you first.

If there is something that you've trialled and implemented as a result of reading this book, we would love to hear from you. It could be a need for improved relationships with your students or perhaps you've gained fresh ideas to assist your teaching practice or new ways to respectfully connect with your Aboriginal students and families.

Often when we read a book, we feel inspired to make change so it's now your time to do just that. We wrote this book because we want to make a difference and we hope we've been able to make a difference to your life or teaching practice.

From the bottom of our hearts, we want to thank you for coming on this journey with us. Thank you for your time and dedication to learn and grow to become the best you can be for the young people in your life.

If someone hasn't told you lately, we're here to tell you that you are valued and needed. Our young people need you! Each and every one of them have crossed paths with you for a reason. As Rita Pierson says, "We're educators, we can do this, we're born to make a difference".

We'd love to hear from you, so please feel free to email us at info@dreambigedu.com.au or via social media. We didn't write this book for us; we wrote it hoping to support the wonderful work of teachers. We're lifelong learners. We will continue to learn and grow in order to be that teacher who makes a difference.

We'll leave with you with a few quotes and words to remind you of how deadly teaching is (the word deadly has been used

Summary

throughout this book and in case you didn't know it means AWESOME, INCREDIBLE, AMAZING – that's you!

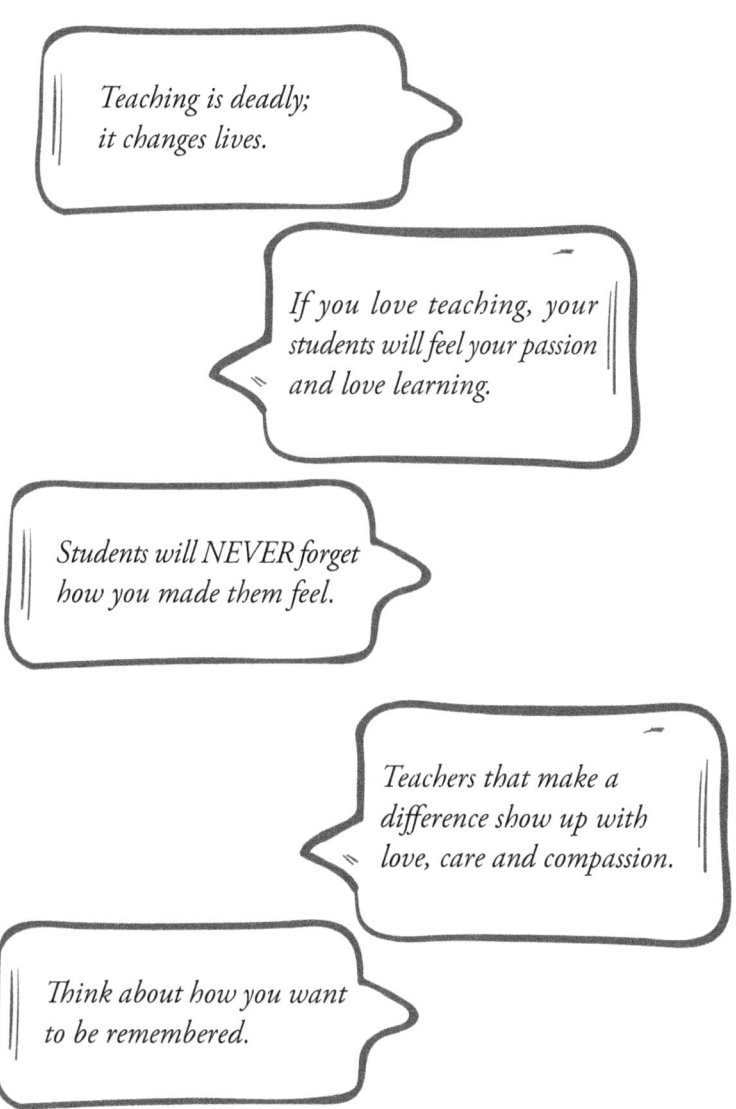

Teaching is deadly; it changes lives.

If you love teaching, your students will feel your passion and love learning.

Students will NEVER forget how you made them feel.

Teachers that make a difference show up with love, care and compassion.

Think about how you want to be remembered.

> Education changes lives, it offers freedom and choice.

> Every human was shaped in some way by a teacher.

> Positive teachers + positive classroom = engaged and positive learners.

> Once you know, you can't unknow.

> Remember, you can't be that teacher if you don't take care of YOU first.

> Teaching is tough but you are tougher.

Summary

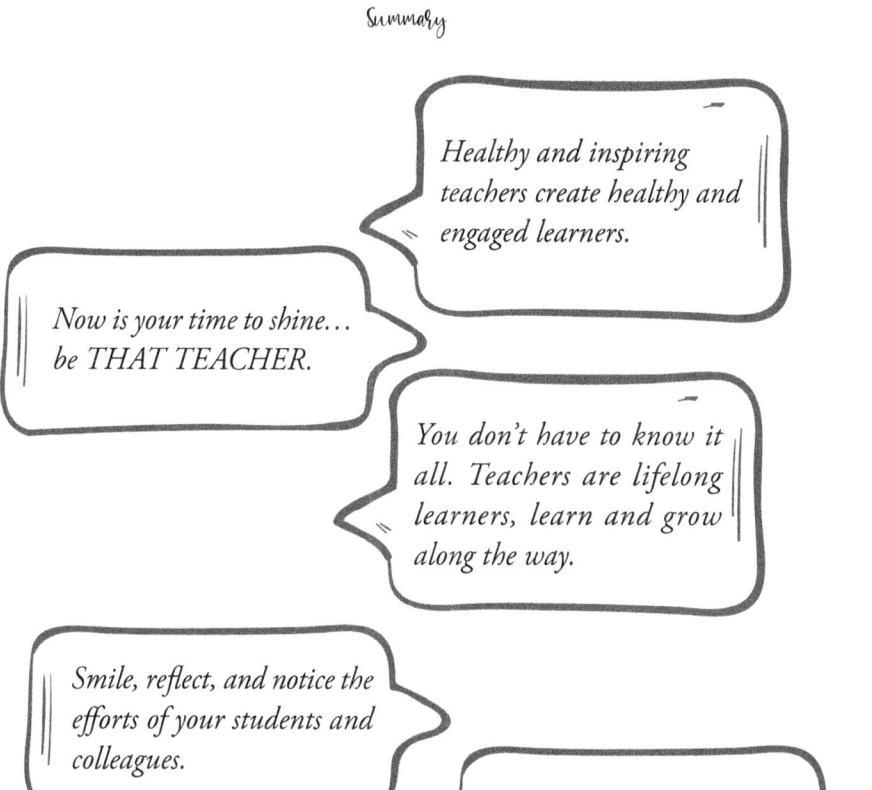

Be deadly and make change!

Take a few moments to journal and create a plan of action moving forward.

What are some actions you can take as a result of reading this book?

_____

_____

_____

_____

_____

Write about an instance where relationships in the classroom have made a difference to learning.

_____

_____

_____

_____

_____

_____

_____

Summary

Can you identify key moments or circumstances that facilitated this instance? Do they suggest a replicable disposition, trend or strategy?

_____

_____

_____

_____

_____

_____

How can you make your students and families feel more valued and acknowledged?

_____

_____

_____

_____

_____

_____

Identify curriculum changes that you can make to your teaching programs.

_____

_____

_____

_____

_____

What pedagogical strategies might you try to better engage your students in their learning?

_____

_____

_____

_____

_____

Summary

Identify three resources that will support your learning.

_____

_____

_____

_____

_____

Identify three resources that will support student learning.

_____

_____

_____

_____

_____

_____

Identify three attributes a leader needs in schools today.

_____

_____

_____

_____

_____

Reflect on what type of leader you wish to be in the field of Aboriginal education.

_____

_____

_____

_____

_____

Summary

Map out a school reform strategy that centres Country and Aboriginal voices in a new vision for the school.

_____

_____

_____

_____

_____

How and where can you find joy in your teaching?

_____

_____

_____

_____

_____

_____

Fast forward to the end of your career and write a letter reflecting on the wonderful career you've had, focussing on the difference you've made to countless numbers of students. How do you want to be remembered? What will be said at your retirement celebration?

_____

_____

_____

_____

_____

_____

_____

_____

_____

_____

_____

_____

ABOUT THE AUTHORS

Associate Professor Cathie Burgess

Associate Professor Cathie Burgess is a lecturer/researcher in Aboriginal Studies/Education, Aboriginal Community Engagement, Learning from Country and Leadership in Aboriginal Education programs at the Sydney School of Education and Social Work, The University of Sydney. Her extensive expertise in this area is built on 25 years teaching and leadership experience in secondary schools in Aboriginal Studies, Aboriginal curriculum and pedagogies across key learning areas, and innovative literacy strategies to improve student outcomes. Cathie's Aboriginal Issues Blackline Masters series of ten books continues to be popular in primary and secondary schools today.

Cathie maintains strong connections with schools across the state through her university teaching and research activities as well as advocating for Aboriginal Studies at local and national levels. As President of the Aboriginal Studies Association NSW for 13 years, and now Vice President, Cathie conducts high-level professional learning for local, interstate and international educators. Cathie's work in Aboriginal Education and Aboriginal Studies is acknowledged by being awarded Honorary Life Member, NSW Aboriginal Education Consultative Group and Life Member, Aboriginal Studies Association NSW.

Cathie's research supports her professional learning expertise which involves community-led initiatives positioning Country, Aboriginal voices, community educators and Elders as leaders and collaborators in curriculum, pedagogy, teacher professional learning, educational leadership and research. Significantly, the Learning from Country in the City teaching/research project is transformative for graduate teachers entering the teaching profession and is the cornerstone of the Aboriginal Voices Culturally Nourishing Schooling Project.

About the Authors

Kylie Captain

Kylie Captain is a proud Gamilaroi woman, educator and author, born and raised in the inner-city Sydney suburbs of Redfern and Waterloo. Kylie's family is from Walgett, a small country town in North West New South Wales.

Kylie's recently published book, *Dream Big and Imagine the What If,* and accompanying journal is making a difference in the lives of many across Australia and abroad.

Kylie is the President of the Aboriginal Studies Association and, over the past 22 years, has had an impressive career in education, finance and community service. Kylie studied a Bachelor of Education (Primary) - Aboriginal and Torres Strait Islander Education. She currently works closely with educators around curriculum implementation through the delivery of professional learning and strategic support to improve Aboriginal education. Kylie is a sought-after speaker and facilitator and has been the keynote speaker at prestigious events across the nation.

In her book, Kylie shares her story of loss and circumstance. With an honest and powerful voice, she explains how a teacher helped her find the strength and inspiration to overcome the challenges she encountered to now enjoy a full and abundant life. Kylie's story is a testament to the strength of culture, kin and connection to Country. She shares her experience and knowledge as an educational leader and through her narrative, takes you on an eye-opening journey of truth-telling, identity and hope. From breaking the cycle and facing fear to using the power of education and visualisation, Kylie inspires many to take on life's challenges with strength and courage.

Kylie's dream is to pay it forward by sharing her love of education in hope that every student will know that they too can achieve anything they set their mind to. She dedicates her life to improving outcomes for Aboriginal students and inspiring anyone to recognise their potential, believe in themselves and chase their dreams.

WANT MORE?

- Enquire about a 'Be That Teacher' masterclass based on the themes of this book. Contact Kylie and Cathie via the contact form at https://www.kyliecaptain.com.au/ or email info@dreambigedu.com.au

- To purchase a copy of Dream Big and Imagine the What If or the Dream Big Journal by Kylie Captain, head to https://www.kyliecaptain.com.au/

- Further copies of this book can also be purchased by visiting the website above.

- Download your free Teacher Reflection Journal by visiting the store at kyliecaptain.com.au

- Keep an eye out for webinars or professional learning events run by Kylie and Cathie on social media or sign up to our mailing list by visiting Kylie's website.

- Kylie specialises in public speaking, Aboriginal cultural education and inspiring student and teacher workshops focussed on curriculum, wellbeing and resilience.

- Cathie specialises in developing deeper conceptual understandings and practical applications of curriculum, pedagogy, resources and leadership.

- Follow Kylie and Cathie on social media.

- Follow the Aboriginal Studies Association on Twitter or join the Facebook Group by searching 'Aboriginal Studies Association'.

- Become a member of the Aboriginal Studies Association via https://www.aboriginalstudies.com.au/

FURTHER TESTIMONIALS

A good teacher who cares for you as a student and your learning is so important. You never ever forget your good teachers. Teachers have the ability to engage the minds of Deadly young people and foster their interests so they can go on to achieve their dreams. Educators are at the battle face. Good teachers foster good people. Love to all the teachers.

Corey Tutt OAM
Author/CEO/Founder/Director and
Proud Gamilaraay man
DeadlyScience Ltd

Cathie's mentoring radically changed my classroom practice and equipped me to make a difference in schools. Her experience as teacher and educator rises above the cacophony of voices in Aboriginal education.

Linda ten Kate
Educational Leader

We as educators join the teaching profession to make a difference. As co-authors, Kylie sharing through student voice and Cathie sharing through her 40+ years of educational leadership gives the practicality to creating a sense of belonging, building trust through relationships and connecting with students, families and communities to "be that teacher who makes a difference" for new, early career or experienced educators.

The stories shared are a true reflection of how a significant other can impact and change the trajectory for students whilst providing an opportunity for reflection and prompting questions of current practice for those educators ready to make change.

Kylie has once again shared her story through raw and honest dialogue and together with Cathie have created a platform for educators to consider student purpose, how to create opportunities for success and inspire in their goals and aspirations.

Both are exceptional leaders and it is a must read for anyone supporting children and young people.

I am so proud of Kylie's bravery to share her story through another lens, to call her a sista, valued friend and colleague.

Sherrie Meyers
Aboriginal Educational Leader

Further Testimonials

From the instant I met Kylie at a parent/teacher interview I knew she would be a long-standing friend and valued colleague. Having taught her incredible son Tyrell, and later, nephew Jayden, this offered us the strong foundation for some highly aspirational and rigorous dialogue around Aboriginal Education. When Kylie told me all those years ago that she was thinking about enrolling into primary education, I couldn't respond quickly enough as I knew she would make a momentous and instrumental contribution to education. Her impact and phenomenally humble and vibrant, uplifting energy is infectious; exactly what we need in Aboriginal Education moving forward! Her projection and exponential rise to leadership in this sphere was inevitable and speaks volumes to her powerful and unwavering drive and passion.

I feel honoured to have been asked to provide a testimonial and am humbled at the opportunity to express my gratitude to both Kylie and Cathie on their enduring contribution to Aboriginal Studies over the decades. As a non-Aboriginal teacher, I have wholeheartedly dedicated the past twelve years to Aboriginal Education and changing the narrative for my deadly students, their families and indeed the wider school community. I am eternally grateful for their wisdom, integrity, guidance and encouragement of me and the endless knowledge they share through this book to continue to inspire other teachers … especially in a climate where our profession is metaphorically "drowning" in a sea of demands, expectations and pressures.

A million thanks for investing in us and sharing so generously your expertise and enveloping us in your stories and treasure chest filled with golden gifts!

In solidarity always,

Marea Soulos
Aboriginal Studies Teacher

This book reminds us of the awesome power we have in shaping the future of our society. As teachers, we are the difference in a child's life and we have an incredible responsibility in encouraging, supporting and championing the little people that come into our classrooms every day. Caring for our students and teachers and wanting them to achieve their every dream is what we wake up for every morning. This book is the how-to guide to support, uplift, motivate and inspire. Kylie demonstrates extraordinary leadership in all areas, and her story should be the constant reminder that our students possess amazing gifts that are ready to be unwrapped!

Donna Barton
Educational Leader

Firstly, I would like to congratulate Kylie and Cathie on writing this book. The topic they are sharing is such an important one for so many, but in particular, our young people going through the schooling system. It is so important for teachers to realise they are huge role models to our children and really have a big role in shaping their future.

Through personal experience, I know how important it is because I have witnessed someone very close to me lose hope, begin disliking himself, turning to bad choices, attempting suicide and really battling to find out who he is.

This change in him occurred during his secondary education with a teacher and it didn't matter what I did, I couldn't undo the damage at the time. It has taken a lot of years and we still have a lot of work ahead to show him how amazing he is.

I really love this book and the message of passionate teachers and remembering why they entered the profession. It is so vitally important to not only them enjoying their roles, but to the young people they are teaching and guiding.

Congratulations Kylie and Cathie on a wonderful book that so many will enjoy and learn about things we otherwise may not have a chance to.

Julie Fisher
Author

ACRONYMS

Acronym	Expanded Version	Description
ABC	Australian Broadcasting Commission	An independent statutory authority established under the Australian Broadcasting Corporation Act 1983 broadcasting radio and television to Australia in competition with commercial broadcasters.
ACARA	Australian Curriculum and Assessment and Reporting Authority	National body that designs curriculum for states and territories to develop their curriculum.

Acronym	Expanded Version	Description
AECG	Aboriginal Education Consultative Group	This Aboriginal organisation is the peak education body for liaising with the government.
AEO (AEW)	Aboriginal Education Officer (Worker)	Paraprofessionals employed in schools to support Aboriginal students, families and help teachers develop curriculum.
AIATSIS	Australian Institute of Aboriginal and Torres Strait Islander Studies	Australia's only national institution focused exclusively on the diverse history, cultures and heritage of Aboriginal and Torres Strait Islander Australia.
ASA	Aboriginal Studies Association	Professional teacher association supporting teachers and community implementing Aboriginal studies and curriculum content.

Acronyms

Acronym	Expanded Version	Description
CCP	Cross Curriculum Priority – in this document – specifically the Aboriginal and Torres Strait Islander Cross Curriculum Priority	One of three Cross Curriculum Priorities in the Australian Curriculum that is applied to all teaching areas.
HSC	Higher School Certificate	Final exams in schools in NSW largely used to attain marks for university.
KLA	Key Learning Area	Areas of study that the curriculum is divided up into.
LFC	Learning from Country	A teaching/learning approach that positions Aboriginal people and Country front, centre and foundation.
NAIDOC	National Aboriginal & Islander Day of Celebration	Celebrates the history, culture and achievements of Aboriginal and Torres Strait Islander peoples annually.

Acronym	Expanded Version	Description
NIAAA	National Indigenous Artists Advocacy Association	This is a non-profit organisation dedicated to protecting Aboriginal and Torres Strait Islander rights, cultures, protocols and values.
PISA	Programme for International Student Assessment	International assessment tests in OECD countries that compare national benchmarks for literacy, numeracy and science between countries.
SBS	Special Broadcasting Service	An independent statutory authority established under the Special Broadcasting Service Act 1991 broadcasting diverse, multicultural radio and television.

WORKS BY DR CATHIE BURGESS

Video Productions

2022 Learning from Country in the City teaching/research project

- Explaining LFC   **https://youtu.be/GvnJSqGZOI8**

- LFC Experiences   **https://youtu.be/9f70k-peyMo**

- Relationship building **https://youtu.be/5v-SnEC1UFc**

- **2017** Aboriginal Studies Association NSW President (**https://www.youtube.com/watch?v=lu6IMftdNuA**)

- **2017** Aboriginal Community Engagement (**https://www.youtube.com/watch?v=m5CGAlL9M1A**)

Journal Articles, Book Chapters, Information Papers

Aboriginal-led professional learning - Learning from Country

Burgess C. (2022) Learning from Country: Aboriginal Community-Led Relational Pedagogies. In: Peters M.A. *(eds) Encyclopedia of Teacher Education.* Springer, Singapore. https://doi.org/10.1007/978-981-13-1179-6_474-1

Burgess, C., Thorpe, K., Egan, S., & Harwood, V. (2022a) Developing an Aboriginal Curriculum Narrative. *Curriculum Perspectives.* https://doi.org/10.1007/s41297-022-00164-w

Burgess, Thorpe, Egan & Harwood (2022b.) Towards a conceptual framework for Country-inspired teaching and learning *Teachers and Teaching. Theory into Practice.*

Burgess, C., & Harwood, V. (2021). Aboriginal cultural educators teaching the teachers. Mobilising a collaborative cultural mentoring program to affect change. *Australian Educational Researcher.* https://doi.org/10.1007/s13384-021-00493-1

Thorpe, K., Burgess, C., & Egan, S. (2021). Aboriginal Community-led Preservice Teacher Education: Learning from Country in the City. *Australian Journal of Teacher Education, 46*(1). Retrieved from https://ro.ecu.edu.au/ajte/vol46/iss1/4

Burgess, C., Bishop, M., & Lowe, K. (2020). Decolonising Indigenous education. The case for cultural mentoring in supporting Indigenous knowledge reproduction. *Discourse: The cultural politics of education.* https://doi.org/10.1080/01596306.2020.1774513

Burgess, C. (2019). Beyond cultural competence: Transforming teacher professional learning through Aboriginal community-controlled cultural immersion. *Critical Studies in Education, 60*(4). pp477- 495

Burgess, C., Cavanagh, P. (2016). Cultural Immersion: Developing a Community of Practice of Teachers and Aboriginal Community Members. *The Australian Journal of Indigenous Education*, 45(1), 48-55.

Burgess, C., & Cavanagh, P. (2013). *Opening Up To Local Communities. 'You must have a heart miss, none of them other teachers ever go there'*. Final Report of the External Research Team on the implementation of the Connecting to Country Program. Darlinghurst Sydney: Department of Education and Communities. Retrieved from: https://education.nsw.gov.au/about-us/educational-data/cese/evaluation-evidence-bank/reports/implementation-of-the-connecting-to-country-program-final-report

Culturally Nourishing Schooling Project

Moodie, N., Lowe, K., Dixon, R., Trimmer, K. (eds) (2022). *Assessing the Evidence in Indigenous Education Research: Implications for Policy and Practice*. Palgrave Macmillan, Cham. (See chapters 1, 2, 3, 6, 7, 9, 12, 13)

Burgess, C., Frycker A., & Weuffen, S. (2022). Lessons to learn, discourses to change, relationships to build: How Decolonising Race Theory can articulate the interface between school leadership and Aboriginal students' schooling experiences. *Australian Educational Researcher* https://doi.org/10.1007/s13384-022-00546-z

Frycker A., Moodie, N., & Burgess, C. (2023). 'Why can't we be smart?' Exploring School Community partnerships through Decolonising Race Theory. *Australian Educational Researcher*.

Burgess, C. (2021) *Ditching school-based courses cuts passion and wonder. Shame the bureaucrats don't see that*. Blogpost, Australian Association for Research in Education, 28/01/2021. https://www.aare.edu.au/blog/?p=8244

Lowe, K., Tennent, C., Moodie, N., Guenther, J., & Burgess, C. (2021) School-based Indigenous cultural programs and their impact on Australian Indigenous students: a systematic review, *Asia-Pacific Journal of Teacher Education*, 49(1), 78-98, DOI: 10.1080/1359866X.2020.1843137

Burgess, C., & Lowe, K. (2020). Position Paper: *Culturally Responsive Practices and Culturally Nourishing Education*. Evidence for Learning. Social Ventures Australia

Lowe, K., Skrebneva, I., Burgess, C., Harrison, N., & Vass, G. (2020). Towards an Australian model of culturally nourishing schooling. *Journal of Curriculum Studies*. DOI: 10.1080/00220272.2020.1764111

Lowe, K, Skrebneva, I., Harrison, N., Burgess, C., & Moodie. (2020). School-based Indigenous cultural programs and their impact on Australian Indigenous students: A systematic review. *Asia Pacific Journal of Teacher Education*

Burgess, C. (2019). *Effective Teaching Methods in Indigenous Education: the latest research*. Blogpost, Australian Association for Research in Education,15/04/ 2019. https://www.aare.edu.au/blog/?p=3941

Burgess, C., Tennent, C., Vass, G., Guenther, J. Lowe, K., & Moodie, N. (2019). A systematic review of pedagogies that support, engage and improve the educational outcomes of Aboriginal students? *The Australian Educational Researcher*, 46(2), 297-318. Doi 0.1007/s13384-019-00315-5

Lowe, K., Harrison, N., Burgess, C., & Vass, G. (2019) *Summary of recent systematic reviews on Indigenous education: importance of cultural programs in schools; school and community engagement; and school leadership.* Social Ventures Australia 25 October 2019 https://www.socialventures.com.au/assets/SVA-Perspective-Education-Evidence-scan-for-Aboriginal-and-Torres-Strait-Islander-children.pdf

Vass, G., Lowe, K., Burgess, C., Harrison, N. & Moodie, N. (2019). The possibilities and practicalities of professional learning in support of Indigenous student experiences in schooling: A systematic review. *The Australian Educational Researcher*, 46(2), 341-361

Curriculum

Burgess, C., Thorpe, K., Egan, S., & Harwood, V. (2022a.) Developing an Aboriginal Curriculum Narrative. *Curriculum Perspectives.* https://doi.org/10.1007/s41297-022-00164-w

Stern, D., & Burgess, C. (2020). 'Teaching from the Heart'. Challenges for non-Aboriginal teachers teaching Stage 6 Aboriginal Studies in NSW Secondary Schools. *The Australian Journal of Indigenous Education.* 1–8. https://doi.org/10.1017/jie.2020.3

Scarcella, J., & Burgess, C. (2019) Aboriginal perspectives in English classroom texts *English in Australia*, 54(1) 20-29.

Morris, A., & Burgess, C. (2018) The inclusivity and intellectual quality of Aboriginal and Torres Strait Islander content in the NSW History syllabus. *Curriculum Perspectives, 38,* 107-116. Doi:10.1007/s41297-018-0045-y

Burgess, C., & Evans, J. (2017). Culturally responsive relationships focused pedagogies: The key to quality teaching and quality learning environments. In J. Keengwe (Eds.), *Handbook of research on promoting cross-cultural competence and social justice in teacher education.* (pp 1-31). Hershey, PA: IGI Global.

Policy

Burgess, C., & Lowe, K. (2022). Rhetoric vs reality: The disconnect between policy and practice for teachers implementing Aboriginal education in their schools. Education Policy Analysis Archives, 30(97). https://doi.org/10.14507/epaa.30.6175. This article is part of the special issue Teachers and Educational Policy: Markets, Populism, and Im/Possibilities for Resistance, guest edited by Meghan Stacey, Mihajla Gavin, Jessica Gerrard, Anna Hogan and Jessica Holloway. https://protect-au.mimecast.com/s/xXdJC nx1jniGpr5DWS9vleo?domain=epaa.asu.edu

Burgess, C., & Lowe, K. (2019) Aboriginal Voices: Social Justice and Transforming Aboriginal Education. In K. Freebody, S.

Goodwin and H. Proctor. *Higher Education, Pedagogy and Social Justice Politics and Prac*tice. Palgrave McMillan, pp.97-117.

Other

Welsh, J. & Burgess, C. (2021). Trepidation, Trust and Time. Research with Aboriginal communities. In, J. Flexner., V. Rawlings., & L. Riley (Eds). *Community-Led Research: Walking Many Paths Together.* Sydney University Press, pp. 147-168

Burgess, C. Thorpe, K., & Egan, S, (2021. *The role of The Smith Family's Learning for Life educational scholarship program* in supporting *Aboriginal and Torres Strait Islander students complete Year 12.* Unpublished report for The Smith family.

Burgess, C., Thorpe, K., & Egan, S. (2019). *Aboriginal and Torres Strait Islander students early exist from The Smith Family's Learning for Life educational scholarship program. A Report for The Smith Family.*

Burgess, C. (2017). 'Having to say everyday. I'm not black enough…I'm not white enough': Discourses of Aboriginality in the Australian education context. *Race Ethnicity and Education,* 20(6), 737-751.

Burgess, C. (2016). Conceptualising a pedagogical cultural identity through the narrative construction of early career Aboriginal teachers' professional identities. *Teaching and Teacher Education, 58,* 109-118.

REFERENCES

AIATSIS. (2018). The Little Red Yellow Black Book: An introduction to Indigenous Australia (Fourth Edition). AIATSIS.

Australian Curriculum and Assessment and Reporting Authority (version 8.4) *Aboriginal and Torres Strait Islander Cross Curriculum Priority*. https://www.australiancurriculum.edu.au/f-10-curriculum/cross-curriculum-priorities/aboriginal-and-torres-strait-islander-histories-and-cultures/

Australian Curriculum and Assessment and Reporting Authority (2022) The Australian Curriculum (version 9) https://v9.australiancurriculum.edu.au/

Australian Institute of Aboriginal and Torres Strait Islander Studies. (2018). *The Little Red, Yellow and Black Book*. 4th Edition. Aboriginal Studies Press.

Baker, J. (2022). Christian and Western heritage elevated in revised national curriculum, *Sydney Morning Herald* (February 4, 2022). https://www.smh.com.au/education/christian-and-western-heritage-elevated-in-revised-national-curriculum-20220203-p59to1.html#:~:text=A%20revised%20national%20curriculum%20will,subject%20was%20being%20dumbed%20down .

Bodkin-Andrews, G., & Carlson, B. (2014). The legacy of racism and Indigenous Australian identity within education. *Race, Ethnicity and Education*, 19(4), 1-24.

Burarrwanga, Laklak, Ritjilili Ganambarr, Merrkiyawuy Ganambarr-Stubbs, Banbapuy Ganambarr, Djawundil Maymuru, Sarah Wright, Sandie Suchet-Pearson, and Kate Lloyd. *Welcome to My Country*. Sydney: Allen & Unwin, 2013.

Burgess, C., & Cavanagh, P. (2013*). Opening Up To Local Communities. 'You must have a heart miss, none of them other teachers ever go there'. Final Report of the External Research Team on the implementation of the Connecting to Country Program*. Darlinghurst Sydney: Department of Education and Communities. Retrieved November 3, 2015, from http://www.cese.nsw.gov.au/ evaluation-repository-search/opening-up-to-localcommunities-connecting-to-country-project.

Burgess, C., Tennent, C., Vass, G., Guenther, J. Lowe, K., & Moodie, N. (2019). A systematic review of pedagogies that support, engage and improve the educational outcomes of Aboriginal students? *The Australian Educational Researcher, 46*(2), 297-318. Doi 0.1007/s13384-019-00315-5

Burgess, C., Thorpe, K., Egan, S., & Harwood, V. (2022a) Developing an Aboriginal Curriculum Narrative. *Curriculum Perspectives.* https://doi.org/10.1007/s41297-022-00164-w

Burgess, C., Thorpe, K., Egan, S., & Harwood, V. (2022b.) Toward a conceptual framework for Country-inspired teaching and learning. T*eachers and Teaching. Theory into Practice.* https://doi.org/10.1080/13540602.2022.2137132

Commonwealth Government. (2007). *Aboriginal Affairs background notes : The history of Aboriginal land rights in Australia*, AGPS R84/80 Cat. No. 84 145 6

Donnelly, K., & Wiltshire, K. (2014). *Review of the national curriculum: Final report.* https://docs.education.gov.au/system/files/doc/other/review_of_the_national_curriculum_final_report.pdf.

Dudgeon, P., Wright, M., Paradies, Y., Garvey, D., & Walker, (2014). Aboriginal Social, Cultural and Historical Contexts. In P. Dudgeon, H. Milroy & R. Walker. *Working Together: Aboriginal and Torres*

Strait Islander Mental Health and Wellbeing Principles and Practice. (pp. 3-24). Barton, ACT: Commonwealth of Australia.

Early Childhood Australia. (2014). Pedagogy, Programs and Practice. https://www.earlychildhoodaustralia.org.au/our-publications/research-practice-series/research-practice-series-index/2014-issues/pedagogy-programs-relationships-practice/

Education Council. (2019). *Alice Springs (Mparntwe) Education Declaration*. Carlton South, Victoria: Education Services Australia.

Healing Foundation (2014). *Stolen Generations Resource Kit for Teachers and Students.* https://healingfoundation.org.au/schools/

Kennedy, A. (2014). *Pedagogy: Programs and relationships in practice.* Early Childhood Australia.

Ladwig.J., Gore.J., Amaosa.W., & Griffiths.T. (2009) 'Quality Teaching Matters' Issue 27 in *'Side by Side'*. NSW Department of Education and Training

Lowe, K., & Yunkaporta, T. (2013). The inclusion of Aboriginal and Torres Strait Islander content in the Australian National Curriculum: A cultural, cognitive and socio-political evaluation. *Curriculum Perspectives, 33*(1), 1-14.

Martin, K. (2005). Childhood, lifehood and relatedness: Aboriginal ways of being, knowing and doing. In J. Phillips and J. Lampert. *Introductory Studies in Education.* pp. 27-40. Pearson Education Australia.

McGaw, B. (2014) Options Not Orders. *Sydney Morning Herald* (February 27, 2014). Retrieved https://www.smh.com.au/opinion/crosscurriculum-priorities-are-options-not-orders-20140226-33iae.html]

NSW Department of Education (2003) *NSW Quality Teaching Framework. Classroom Discussion.* https://theelements.schools.nsw.gov.au/introduction-to-the-elements/policy-reforms-and-focus-areas/quality-teaching-framework.htm

NSW Education Standards Authority (2020). *Aboriginal Studies 7-10 Syllabus.* https://educationstandards.nsw.edu.au/wps/portal/nesa/k-10/learning-areas/hsie/aboriginal-studies-7-10-2020

Parbury, N. (2005). *Survival: a history of Aboriginal life in New South Wales.* NSW Department of Aboriginal Affairs.

Reconciliation Australia. (n.d). *The Australian Reconciliation Barometer.* https://www.reconciliation.org.au/reconciliation/australian-reconciliation-barometer/

Riley, L., Sebastian, T., & Bowen, B. (2022). *Aboriginal Songlines and the colonial systems of cultural mapping of urban Country through the use of archives, analysis of geographic sites and an exploration of local narratives.* https://issuu.com/opresearch/docs/the_politics_of_design/s/14661460

Soutphommasane, T. (2019). *On hate.* Melbourne University Publishing.

Teach for Australia. (2019). *Australia's 2018 PISA results demonstrate the persistence of gap in achievement for disadvantaged students.* https://teachforaustralia.org/2018-pisa-results-australia-achievement-gap/

Thorpe, K., Burgess, C., & Egan, S. (2021). Aboriginal Community-led Preservice Teacher Education: Learning from Country in the City. *Australian Journal of Teacher Education, 46*(1). https://ro.ecu.edu.au/ajte/vol46/iss1/4

Trimmer, K., Dixon, R., & Guenther, J. (2019). School leadership and Aboriginal student outcomes: Systematic review. *Asia-Pacific Journal of Teacher Education,* 1-17.

Uluru Statement of the Heart: https://ulurustatement.org/the-statement/

Wenger, E. (2000). Communities of practice and social learning systems. *Organization, 7*(2), 225–246.

Yunkaporta, T. (2009). *Aboriginal pedagogies at the cultural interface.* (PhD), James Cook University.

NOTES

www.ingramcontent.com/pod-product-compliance
Lightning Source LLC
Chambersburg PA
CBHW070654120526
44590CB00013BA/950